house for payment transactions indicated six barriers in the social system: the existing division of labour and poor interfunctional teamwork, the norms and values limiting people's ability to change, top-down leadership and poor vertical communication, inadequate management skills, and a linear and formal process of decision making on issues of innovation.

The results of Wastell and Cooper are in a similar direction. They report a comparative analysis of two projects involving the computerization of control room operations in two ambulance services, with strikingly different results. These contrasting outcomes are attributed to two main sets of factors: the design philosophy of the more successful case was "user-centred"; the aim of technological innovation was to support and augment the role of human operator. In contrast, the less successful project appeared to embody a highly Tayloristic philosophy, accentuating the replacement of unreliable human labour by an automated system. In terms of implementation strategy, two features were recognized as critical success factors: top management commitment and user implementation.

Eason, Harker, and Olphert argue that we need methods to support participative and integrative systems development in order to ensure that organizational requirements and options are considered alongside technical opportunities. In their contribution the authors review the methods available for integrative and user-centred work. They conclude that the development of methods has concentrated on approaches that are useful in the implementation phase. However, this is often too late to make major changes. On the other hand, user participation earlier in the development process is often limited to asking users to review abstract technical descriptions in order to judge organizational implications. The authors developed the ORDIT (Organizational Requirements Definition for Information Technology Systems) methodology to provide stronger support for user-centred integrative analysis and design at an early stage. The method provides a mechanism integrating the business process, the social system, and the development of future alternative socio-technical scenarios. It helps stakeholders to understand the implications of technology sufficiently early for them to be able to influence the direction of development. The application of tele-medicine in health care is presented as a case study to demonstrate how this method can be used.

Van Offenbeek and Koopman argue that "user participation" should be viewed in a more differentiated way. They show that, although most system developers nowadays indicate that they accept the necessity of user participation, the daily practice is often different. The authors plead for a switch from the concept of "user participation" to "contingent interaction" among parties involved. They present a contingency model in which five types of risks are described: functional uncertainty, technical uncertainty, conflict potential, resistance potential, and material preconditions. The contingency model specifies the approaches of interaction that are supposed to be more appropriate under each condition. Early results based on seven case studies provide some support for this model.

The final contribution, by Hanappi-Egger, focuses on systems supporting group decision making and co-operative work. She analyses bargaining over work-distribution schemas in professional work groups and investigates how the group dynamic aspects can be modelled in order to design a technical support system. The advantage of such a decision support system is that it allows preferences to be articulated in a more democratic and less threatening way.

The contributions in this issue vary widely in their scope, in the sectors they cover, and in the technical systems involved. There is, however, one similar message to be found throughout all the approaches: It is not the information technology itself that is the crucial factor for quality of work, for workers, or for the organization, but the strategy adopted to integrate the technology in the changing organization. This issue shows that theory and practical methodology of achieving such an integrative approach have progressed substantially over the last decade.

J.H. ERIK ANDRIESSEN
Delft University of Technology,
The Netherlands

PAUL L. KOOPMAN
Free University, Amsterdam,
The Netherlands

CN 303.483
AN 5214

EUROPEAN JOURNAL OF WORK AND ORGANIZATIONAL PSYCHOLOGY, 1996, 5 (3), 321–324

Introduction: People-oriented Introduction of Information and Communication Technology in Organizations

Information Technology (IT) is often associated with issues of data processing and information management through large-scale information systems. However, for the last 10 years IT has not only referred to (1) computer-assisted information processing technologies, but also to (2) computer-assisted communication technologies, and (3) computer-assisted decision support technologies. It is therefore more adequate to speak of Information and Communication Technology (ICT). These advanced forms of IT enable the development of new forms of work and organization, such as distributed teamwork, mobile work, telework, inter-organizational networking, and outsourcing activities to other countries.

Traditional information systems are now being complemented or integrated with decision support systems, expert systems, and what is sometimes called "groupware", i.e. technology supporting, for example, electronic mail, video-conferencing, mobile calling, and flexible command and control systems.

The growth of this form of technology is related to the fact that organizations have to cope with changes in the socio-economic environment. General societal and economic developments increasingly require an international orientation, geographical distribution, and increased flexibility of the production process and workforce. Moreover, fierce competition forces organizations to reduce overhead costs as much as possible. Very few companies can evade the pressure for increased flexibility in production processes and organizational functioning, reflected in phenomena such as "just in time" logistics, decentralization of decision making, and flexibilization or even externalization of labour. Some firms have undertaken a dramatic reordering of the primary processes through what is called "business process redesign". IT is adopted and designed to solve problems caused by these changes.

The implications of these developments for work and workers are only slowly becoming manifest. A widely divergent world of work is dawning in organizations where "mediated co-operative work" plays an important role, in the context of organizational networks, temporary connections, teamwork, and distributed working. In the Book Reviews section a publication is discussed (Howard's *The Changing Nature of Work*) that analyses the potential implications of these changes for work, workers, and working.

Both organizational and technical design issues will be of major import-ance to work and organization. Few work and organizational psychologists are presently involved in the technical design of ICT systems, but this special issue of the *European Journal of Work and Organizational Psychology* shows that their participation in the implementation of these systems in organizations is significant.

Technological and organizational innovation requires a theoretical framework to understand the relationships between strategy, technology, and organization, and to guide the change process. The contributions in this issue discuss the introduction of ICT in the frameworks of what are called integrative analysis, user-oriented design, and socio-technical approaches, in some cases comparing this with "business process redesign". Of course these concepts are not new. New, however, is the refinement of these models, the sophistication of the methodology implied by the approaches, and the application to novel situations such as large-scale tele-informatics. Compared with business process redesign approaches, the methods dis-cussed in this issue seem to have more favourable impacts.

Business process redesign in the insurance and health-care sectors is studied by Willcocks and Currie. They compare their findings with the BPR model for change presented by Hammer and Champy (1993). The cases show that radical re-engineering was applicable in a definable business unit with a relatively simple structure, clear objectives, and where performance and improvement is easily measured. The results also point out conditions under which a unitary perspective on the organization cannot adequately address political and cultural issues. Radical re-engineering offers senior manage-ment the opportunity to "forget the past". In this process human resources are treated largely in mechanistic terms. Difficulties are engendered by overemphasizing the need for transformation, "starting over", and downplaying the role of history and continuity.

Boonstra and Vink argue that contemporary socio-technical system theory provides a better knowledge base for redesigning as well as developing organizations through learning processes. In this respect they see the theory as more mature and helpful than the "loose collection of insights and methods" that make up business process redesign. However, further development of socio-technical system theory is needed according to the authors. In particular, they emphasize the field of strategic develop-ment and issues concerning barriers, power, and influence during funda-mental change processes. They claim that impediments to technological and organizational innovation are seldom related to the technological system. Barriers for innovation and reasons for organizational conservatism are mostly found in the social system. Case research in an automated clearing

EUROPEAN JOURNAL OF WORK AND ORGANIZATIONAL PSYCHOLOGY, 1996, 5 (3), 325–350

Information Technology and Radical Re-engineering: Emerging Issues in Major Projects

Leslie P. Willcocks

Oxford Institute of Information Management, Templeton College, Kennington, Oxford, UK

Wendy L. Currie

Sheffield University Management School, University of Sheffield, Sheffield, UK

The paper examines the findings from longitudinal case study work conducted in the 1992–95 period in two organizations in the United Kingdom insurance and health care sectors. The study highlights the many cultural, political, and technical issues that emerge in the strategy and implementation of large-scale radical re-engineering projects. The radical re-engineering perspective and model for change presented by Hammer and Champy (1993) are compared against empirical findings. These suggest that the Hammer and Champy advice contains many limitations. The cases show the specific circumstances in which radical re-engineering can be effective in managerial terms, but also point to conditions under which a unitary perspective on the organization often cannot address adequately many critical political and cultural issues. Moreover the case histories point to (1) the dangers of an over-reliance on a methodological holism that can be rarely delivered on in complex large-scale organizations, given the scale of change envisaged; and (2) the difficulties engendered by overemphasizing the need for transformation and "starting again", and downplaying the role of history and continuity in both the study and management of organizational change.

INTRODUCTION

Re-engineering, or business process re-engineering (BPR) has been described as the fundamental rethinking and radical redesign of business processes to bring about dramatic improvements in performance (Hammer & Stanton, 1995). A key element is a focus on process—a structured, measured set of activities designed to produce a specified output for a particular customer or market (Davenport, 1993b). The BPR activity described in

---

Requests for reprints should be addressed to L.P. Willcocks, Oxford Institute of Information Management, Templeton College, Kennington, Oxford OX1 5NY, UK.

the literature varies in the scale and type of change contemplated (Heygate, 1993; Morris & Brandon, 1993). Central to BPR practice, according to most sources, is a holistic approach to strategy, structure, process, people, and technology (see for example Galliers, 1994; Hammer & Stanton, 1995; Johannsson, McHugh, Pendlebury, & Wheeler, 1993).

BPR as an analysis, as a set of prescriptions for management, and in practice can be assessed in several ways and at several different levels. A major concern must be to compare the exhortations against what is actually being achieved in BPR programmes. An important issue that arises from surveys, case study research, and also more anecdotal evidence is why, despite the large sums being spent on re-engineering by some high-profile organizations, and a deluge of prescriptive management literature and consultancy activity, BPR so often seems to fail to live up to expectations. Hammer and Champy estimated a 70% failure rate for the radical re-engineering efforts they had observed, though this figure was not rigorously arrived at, and "implied nothing about the expected rate of success or failure of subsequent reengineering efforts" (Hammer & Stanton, 1994). Recent studies show most re-engineering projects consistently falling well short of dramatic or even expected benefits (Bartram, 1992; Hall, Rosenthal, & Wade, 1993; Harvey, 1995; Moad, 1993).

Findings from a 1995 UK survey (Willcocks, 1996) add to this picture. High-risk, radical BPR approaches were generally not being undertaken. One indication of this was the low expenditure, with 43% of medium and large organizations each incurring BPR-related expenditures of under £1 million. Many of the processes being re-engineered seemed to be existing ones to which improvements were being sought rather than those identified as a result of a radical rethink of how the organization needed to be reconfigured and managed. Radical BPR is portrayed as achieving sizeable job losses yet we found that for all completed BPR projects and all types of process, staff redundancies averaged less than 5% of total BPR costs (Willcocks, 1996). Generally, whatever the process being re-engineered, organizations did not seem to be aiming high when they looked for improvements from BPR. Actual improvements being achieved were also relatively low. Very few organizations were achieving what could be called "breakthrough" results. Thus, of the organizations that had completed BPR programmes, if a relatively conservative benchmark of significance of 20% profitability gain, 20% revenue gain, and 10% decrease in costs of doing business is used, only 18% of organizations had achieved significant financial benefits from BPR on all three measures. Organizations were achieving, and in most cases aiming for, tangible improvements rather than radical change. The picture of discontinuous change represented in the BPR literature is not clearly underscored in BPR practice.

We have argued elsewhere, with others, that such less radical approaches, or the way in which espoused radical aims become emergent, incremental improvements, may be related to the difficulties inherent in actually implementing BPR programmes (Currie, 1995; Davenport, 1993a; Grint & Willcocks, 1995; Smith & Willcocks, 1995). One issue only just emerging is the extent to which BPR efforts fail to link closely with business strategy and with effective organizational processes for strategy formulation. Ironically, this is a feature of a number of texts ostensibly concerned with securing the business strategy–BPR linkage (see for example Belmonte & Murray, 1993; Hammer & Champy, 1993; Johannsson et al., 1993; Morris & Brandon, 1993). This has led some to posit the need to go beyond BPR and focus on business systems engineering (Galliers, 1994; Watson, 1995). Further, a prime question raised by the multidisciplinary holism at the heart of BPR study and practice is that of whether there are robust methodologies and tools available to facilitate the outcomes required from BPR activities. The conclusion has been that, despite many approaches, there is an immaturity and lack of integratedness on the methodological front (Earl & Khan, 1994; Klein, 1994).

In case study research in four organizations we found that the methodologies adopted were often partial, and handled some aspects of what should be a holistic approach better than others (Currie & Willcocks, in press; Smith & Willcocks, 1995). Frequently, IT-based change activities have utilized methodologies that focus on information flows and processes, and are based on systems analysis techniques, but in such a way as to marginalize human, social, and political processes and issues (Walsham, 1993; Walton, 1989). Our own UK survey found such predilections often flowing into how IT-enabled, or IT-driven BPR projects were being handled (Willcocks, 1995a). Indeed, what emerges from the BPR literature itself is the frequency with which failure is related, amongst other reasons, to mismanagement of human, social, and political issues and processes (for examples only see Belmonte & Murray, 1993; Buday, 1992; Moad, 1993; for a more detailed commentary on the political aspects and difficulties experienced in BPR see Grint & Willcocks, 1995).

A long stream of research suggests that these risks and difficulties are compounded where, as is usually the case, IT is added to BPR projects and is seen as a critical enabler in the design phase of BPR and in supporting redesigned processes. Recent UK research found that IT expenditure regularly cost between 22% and 36% of total costs on BPR projects, and that a majority of respondent organizations saw IT as a critical enabler of BPR efforts (Currie & Seddon, 1995; Willcocks, 1995b). Such risks are also related significantly to both the size of the project and the "maturity" or newness of the technology being utilized relative to the organization's experience with that technology (Stringer, 1992; Willcocks & Griffiths, 1994).

Faced with this confusing set of findings, arrived at through studies conducted by a range of stakeholders for various purposes and with varying degrees of rigour, it is clear that further research is needed, particularly in the area of radical re-engineering projects. If the majority of organizations have been found to be conducting process improvement, albeit dressed in radical clothes and vocabulary, and if, despite high-profile successes declared in the trade literature, most radical re-engineering disappoints, one needs to investigate in detail the distinctive conditions under which radical re-engineering projects are being carried out. The purpose of this article is to investigate and analyse in detail two such projects, but before doing so we detail the methodological considerations that informed, and were operationalized in, the research process.

RESEARCH METHODOLOGY

The research objective was to develop academically-researched cases that provided some counterpoint to the many under-researched cases found in the literature, all too often prematurely declared by interested stakeholders as examples of success. The aim was not to provide examples of successful or unsuccessful BPR, but rather to investigate in depth the issues that emerged during the course of large-scale re-engineering projects. The research objectives break down into several aspects.

1. We were interested to elicit data from stakeholders on how specific organizations would set about re-engineering key business processes.
2. The research was focused on some of the critical implementation issues in re-engineering programmes and how these related to the original strategic vision in each case.
3. The researchers were keen to develop a longitudinal perspective on large-scale BPR change programmes and to compare the findings with some of the claims of those who advocate re-engineering as "the way forward" for contemporary businesses (Champy, 1995; Hammer & Champy, 1993; Johannsson et al., 1993). For example, the notion that senior managers can engage in a process of "collective forgetting" (Grint, Case, & Willcocks, 1995) and are thus able to redesign the business from a starting point of a "blank sheet of paper". In addition, the espoused view that re-engineering can transform human relations to the extent that power is shifted from superordinate to subordinate, supervisors to coaches, scorekeepers to leaders; and a shift from concern for the boss to concern for the customer (see Hammer & Champy, 1993 and a critique in Grint, 1993). While much of the management literature suggests that the human resource issues in the process and as the endpoint of change are critical, recent survey research discussed later, however, shows how these issues are often overlooked by those in charge of implementing BPR (Willcocks, 1995a). We wished to investigate whether detailed case research substantiated this finding.

4. The two cases chosen were to have a strong IT-enabling aspect to the BPR activity being investigated. This was partly to reflect, and enable the investigation of, the strong correlation posited in the literature between BPR "newness"/effectiveness and the development of appropriate information systems (see Davenport, 1993b; Hammer & Stanton, 1995; O'Hara & Watson, 1995). This selection also enabled us to examine the degree to which information systems (IS) can have a leadership role in BPR, and at what point this may need to be relinquished (as suggested for example by Davenport & Stoddard, 1994). In-depth case studies also enabled investigation of risk issues associated with major IT projects.

5. In both cases the BPR projects at commencement were also explicitly recognized by senior management to be (a) strategic, that is underpinning the organization's business strategy, (b) radical in terms of the organizational and technical innovations embraced by the project, and (c) large scale in terms of the financial and resource implications for the specific organization. This enabled investigation of the claims made in the management literature regarding how radical re-engineering might be conducted, and what it could achieve.

The research adopted a range of qualitative techniques to investigate and construct the case histories. These were systematically applied to each case study to provide a consistent base for analysis.

- Regular participant observation in the events as they occurred.
- Semi-structured interviews, each of between one and one and a half hours in length, with stakeholders from different levels in the organization and with different roles in the BPR process. The objective throughout was to achieve at least a triangulation of viewpoints on events as they developed.
- A focus on the process of changeover periods ranging from two to three years, rather than take an aprocessual "snapshot" of events at a particular moment in time.
- Utilizing detailed internal documentation available in the organizations studied in order to enrich the accounts and explanations arrived at.

To avoid the ahistorical, aprocessual, and acontextual character of much research on organizational change, data-gathering techniques were also focused on organizational history and context, as well as the content, process, and emergent outcomes of change. This approach built on that of Pettigrew and colleagues adopted for the study of major organizational change (Pettigrew, 1985; Pettigrew, Ferlie, & McKee, 1992; Pettigrew & Whipp, 1991), and that of the authors for parallel studies of risk in major IT projects (Currie, 1994; Willcocks & Griffiths, 1994). Finally, for the purposes of analysis, the research utilized a framework developed from studying parallel case and survey research (Smith & Willcocks, 1995; Willcocks, 1995a, 1995b), from reflecting on the case experiences, and from reviewing the extensive literature on BPR and change management. Outcomes seemed to relate to five significant factors:

- pressure to act
- locus of support
- levers for change (intervention points from which to initiate activity)
- themes (focal messages in the rhetoric of change)
- approach (types of technique, degree of participation).

In what follows the two case histories are detailed, as arrived at through applying the research techniques described previously. The five-factor framework is then used to develop a comparative analysis. We then relate the findings to those from parallel survey and case research on BPR practice and risk factors in major IT projects.

CASE 1—RE-ENGINEERING INSURANCE: NATIONAL VULCAN

Context

In 1990 National Vulcan (NV), an autonomous subsidiary of composite insurer Sun Alliance, was the largest UK insurer in engineering, with a 23% share of a £390 million market. However, after a decade of healthy profits, these fell to £6.1m in 1990, and the company recorded its first loss—of £6.3m—in 1991. The appointment of a new chief executive from a non-engineering subsidiary of Sun Alliance in June 1990 brought an external perspective to long-term operational problems exposed by the recessionary climate for which the organization was clearly unprepared. Loss of major customers in this period, including the major defence contractor British Aerospace, added to the sense of crisis within the company.

The company had two main types of product. First, it sold more than 100 different types of insurance policy. By 1991 some 75,000 annually renewable policies had been issued to customers, providing 60% of the company's revenue. The policies covered engineering risks such as explosion of boilers, physical injury, and damage to third-party property. NV also sold policies covering clients' computer installations. Sales were through the Sun Alliance sales network, its own 24 branches, and professional broking intermediaries specializing in the engineering sector. Second, NV provided a site safety inspection service, available separately, but more often tied in with an NV insurance policy. Here many customers also required annual safety certification to meet statutory safety regulations on items such as electrical equipment, elevators, boilers, and heavy machinery. A wide range of customers included most of the UK's nuclear power stations, several multi-nationals, and also medium-sized companies and their offices, retail outlets, and factories. Some 2.5 million inspections a year resulted in the creation and issuing to clients of nearly half a million written reports.

Internal reviews of the company commissioned by the new chief executive, Ken Sinfield, revealed lack of significant investment, underdeveloped computer-based systems, departments operating in isolation from one another, overelaborate bureaucratic procedures, and staff operating through 55 job grades. A commissioned survey on customer service relative to its competitors revealed NV as bottom. While inspection engineers were rated as best in the sector, and the inspection service contributed 40% of NV revenue, its cost structure was far too high and typically a report took two months to deliver to the client. The insurance business was more open to the fluctuating risk of claims, but on the more controllable cost side was highly inefficient. Issuing a new policy, for example, passed through 43 steps, 20 members of staff, and 10 departments. An even more serious problem identified in the review was the lack of a sense of crisis amongst the workforce. From a chief executive perspective:

> One hundred and thirty years as market leader had bred complacency and introversion . . . people did not have a sense of imminent death . . . we had become a prisoner of our own history [of] technical excellence . . . when it was put to a group of managers that we were in a crisis one perplexed reply was "I don't know what has changed, we haven't."

Identifying Core Processes and the Role of IT

Sinfield determined on a top-down approach incorporating stretch goals for changes in performance. A thorough analysis, by consultants and internal management, of the company's operations and its relations with its customers detailed significant weaknesses. Across all operations little was completed within a three-month cycle. Typically, however, an item was worked on for only three days of the cycle and only three hours of that time provided what Sinfield came to call "the valuable difference" that is added value for the customer. It also became clear that the company was overdependent on paper-based manual operations, many of which were ripe for automation.

In more detail, in the inspection service one or more of the 521 inspection engineers would be assigned to a particular client order. The time taken on subsequent administrative procedures, and the engineers' high involvement in these, was identified as troubling. Engineers used one of 400 available forms to produce a typed report with seven carbon copies. These would be batched twice a week and sent to the Manchester Head Office. There each report was checked by an acceptance engineer, a task that took only a few minutes. However, a backlog of several months had developed; moreover, if a report had inaccuracies it had to be returned to the inspection engineer

5217

for further checking. In the insurance policy area, each insurance policy passed through 30 different checks in 10 departments before insurance cover was authorized. These checks applied to all policies regardless of value and complexity. Despite this level of detail NV could not produce accurate data to identify the profitable and loss-making product lines and clients. Lack of management information could be partly explained by limited experience with IT. The only significant operational IT was the plant database held on an IBM mainframe shared with other Sun Alliance operating companies, and based remotely at Bristol. The NV database contained 1.7 million items. The procedure for updating information was elaborate, there was high staff turnover and wide use of temporary staff, all of which contributed to a high level of data inaccuracy. Finally, NV had too many sales offices for a company of its size; moreover, many were too small to carry out the many different functions ranging from sales generation, handling customer enquiries, policy issuing and service, and debtor control.

A top management team redeveloped the business strategy in early 1991. The mission was to restore profitability and customer confidence through becoming "the highest quality, lowest cost operator in the UK engineering sector" (internal document). A key aspect was radical process redesign. The underlying approach to activity analysis is summarized in Fig. 1.

Beyond this, three key processes and actions were identified. These were:

(a) streamlining the insurance process involving the branch offices and policy administration
(b) upgrading the plant database process involving responding to customer enquiry, updating the database, and scheduling field inspections
(c) simplifying and improving the speed and quality of the report process involving engineers carrying out inspections and making reports, and report delivery to customers.

TYPE OF ACTIVITY	ACTION/SOURCING
1. 'Idle Time' ⟶	Eliminate
2. Unnecessary ⟶	Eliminate
3. Necessary ⟶	IT Enabled/Packages and Outsourced
4. Added Value ⟶	Insourced

FIG. 1.   Identifying added-value activities.

The management team identified IT as a critical enabler of process redesign. The IT manager supported these developments. He had spent some three years at NV with a mandate to improve IT but, in a cost-cutting culture, had not received appropriate support from either the wider Sun Alliance IT community or NV senior management. The new management asked for and received from its loss-making holding company scope for an IT development budget of £6.5m over two years, on top of an ongoing annual operating budget of £2m. However, IT was to follow rather than lead; according to one IT manager:

> First we had to define very clear business goals. Then we defined the processes that flowed from them . . . only then did we go anywhere near IT.

Making Change the Priority

From a senior management perspective, an important means for pushing through change was the setting of "stretch" performance goals. A 24-hour target for the key activity area was insisted on, whether the activity be policy issue, database update, or report despatch. Moreover, whenever a customer contacted the organization only one NV person would be responsible for processing the subsequent transaction. Both goals were counter-cultural and widely perceived amongst middle management and staff to be too difficult to achieve. Senior management responded by heading up some project teams with more junior staff who were supportive of changes. Moreover, project teams were forced to think radically and produce radical solutions by the continuous insistence on getting key processes down to the 24-hour target. The other factor designed to speed progress, maintain enthusiasm, and focus effort was the time-scale set for change. To keep this to a minimum the three IT-enabled process re-engineering projects were to run in parallel, not sequentially. In the first six months, and despite lack of in-house development expertise, senior management made the decision to bypass readily available and stable IT and go with emerging distributed client-server technologies, enabling the company to follow rapid but revolutionary development paths.

Short time-scales were explicitly applied to the restructuring of the sales network. Sales branches were reduced from 26 to nine, and in a nine-week period 138 key people were relocated to a central service unit (CSU) in Manchester. Under a former sales manager from Liverpool branch office, by 1992 the CSU consisted of 300 staff, including 80 from outside the company. Lower-level staff in closed branches were made redundant but the key staff, including branch managers, were assigned to Manchester to retain local knowledge and customer contact. Throughout this process customer service levels actually improved and existing business was retained.

Three major IT-related projects were set up, with a tight nine-month time-scale set for each. The existing two-person computing unit was supplemented by consultants and new full-time IT staff. Additionally, business managers were put in control of the projects. One major project was to develop systems based on Sun workstations and Ingres software to support the insurance administration process. This was achieved in nine months by a nine-person development team, despite software delivery problems due to the supplier experiencing financial difficulties. (Difficulties at NV were also experienced with Wang equipment delivery, for similar reasons.) Ultimately the integrated system enabled a single person at a branch to quote, follow all steps through a single screen, and issue a policy within 24 hours (Fig. 2). Details would then be transmitted overnight to the CSU for subsequent administration, including printing and mailing of policies.

A second nine-person team developed, and transferred the existing records onto, a new Wang-based plant database. The design reduced the updating procedure to two steps, the process became paperless, and the previously high levels of labour turnover amongst plant database operating staff were greatly reduced (see Fig. 2). A further project saw inspection engineers issued with notebook computers supported by software that formatted data automatically and offered flexible layouts and pro-forma

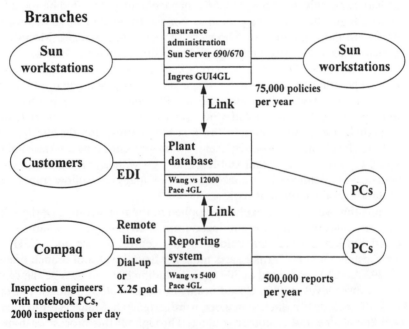

FIG. 2.   IT-enabled re-engineering at National Vulcan.

facilities. This was backed by four days' training in notebook use for every inspection engineer. Reports could be despatched nightly to the Manchester CSU via a modem link, while engineers also had access to the plant database. Only one in 20 reports now needed checking, and this was done on screen, rather than manually. As at 1995 any dialogue with the inspection engineers is achieved electronically and nearly all reports are sent to customers within 24 hours. CSU staffing of the area has been reduced from 140 to 12, and inspection engineer productivity was not only enhanced but also, for the first time, could be monitored accurately.

Subsequent Developments

These re-engineering activities experienced a number of difficulties. Some of the systems identified as necessary but not adding customer value (see Fig. 1) had been outsourced to suppliers, including the business analysis and consultancy aspects of systems development. Vendors proved too responsive to every user request resulting in expensive systems having more functionality than was really required and so the business analysis and consultancy functions were brought back in-house. As the CSU became increasingly IT driven, new processes required older ex-branch personnel to replace their old skills at dealing with brokers and clients with those of team management, a set of skills for which they were ill-equipped. Branches were reducing their numbers by half at a time when Manchester CSU was also reducing staff from 300 to 155 by summer 1993 (and to 75 by mid-1994). Tensions and staff reductions put the 24-hour turnaround target at risk. In early 1993 the CSU was reorganized into a key account team dealing with the top 2000 policies in terms of financial value, and regional teams each dealing with specific branches. However, tensions continued between the CSU and branches, with the latter believing the CSU too remote from customer service. In the CSU morale fell in the face of all these changes, particularly amongst older staff faced with rising skill demands. Turnaround times fell to three days for a period, as greater loads fell on the CSU staff from the downsized branches. Amongst the inspection engineers some frustration was felt at lack of ongoing IT training, and role isolation. By winter 1993, inspection engineers were being grouped into teams of 10 under a senior engineer responsible for appraising performance and training needs. Subsequently, NV has undertaken more widespread training for software packages and PC use amongst CSU staff as well as for inspection engineers. Additionally NV have moved much more towards pay for performance criteria in their reward system, higher accountability amongst staff, and wider adoption of performance appraisal.

Many of these dips in morale could be explained by transition problems, the huge cultural and skills shifts required, and the challenges presented through the lack of IT experience throughout the company. From a chief executive perspective middle management in particular presented the major barrier to the changes envisaged, as Ken Sinfield (quoted in Harvey, 1995), explains:

> I am under no illusion about middle management problems . . . it will take us years . . . I have great sympathy with middle management, but they have got to get in the lifeboat and row with us or we've got a problem.

In this statement one can gain not only some insight into the political and cultural issues prevalent in this re-engineering programme but also, in the language, a sense of the crisis the Chief Executive attempted to communicate to the NV workforce.

Despite these difficulties National Vulcan reported a £4.5m profit in 1993, rising to £9m in 1994. By mid-1995 its staff had been reduced by 25% from its 1991 figure of 1341. This had been achieved mainly through early retirement and voluntary redundancy. Customer complaints were negligible, and productivity of inspection engineers had doubled. As at mid-1995 the company was developing its strategy for the next six years. According to senior management, future changes would have wider staff involvement than in the top-down approach adopted throughout the business process re-engineering programme from 1991.

CASE 2—RE-ENGINEERING IN HEALTH CARE: THE JOHN RADCLIFFE HOSPITAL

Context

This case is set in the 1990–94 period in a major acute hospital—the John Radcliffe (JRH)—in the UK National Health Service (NHS). From the mid-1980s, the NHS was the subject of radical management and organizational reforms prompted by central government. One major feature was the introduction of general managers, and private sector management practice, into hierarchically based administrative structures replete with occupational and professional groupings. A related resource management initiative sought to introduce mechanisms to identify and improve performance in this area. Government also increased pressures to control NHS spending, and sought to develop an internal market in health care. This involved devolution of responsibility for service delivery and increased competition amongst service providers, for example hospitals. These reforms came together in the implementation of a purchaser–provider split across the NHS, accompanied by radical changes in the basis of allocation of finance to purchasers. Henceforth cash-constrained purchasers would seek the most cost-effective health care whether from NHS or private sector providers.

The NHS reforms made sound financial performance a critical issue for hospitals, such as the one under study. Here a number of critical success factors were identified for operating in the new NHS environment. Financial net income had to be maximized. This made efficiency in resource management, together with accurate costing and activity information, crucial. At the same time hospital reputation, standards of care, and staff morale had to be maintained, a broad case-mix was necessary for teaching-hospital purposes, and timely and detailed clinical and audit information was needed to maintain and improve clinical performance.

Earlier top-down reforms of the structure, breaking hierarchically based administration into clinical directorates, only partially worked. It was recognized that a bottom-up approach was needed. The response in late 1990 was to begin a pilot BPR project, facilitated by external consultants. A lead clinician was identified in each of six pilot areas, for example radiology and cardiac services. Each clinician then led a multidisciplinary team to identify the core clinical processes in its own area. In each case there were identified up to 20 processes with a definable start and finish, and for which resources—own and bought in—could be defined and measured. The pilot study proved successful and BPR concepts, together with the pilot way of working, were then applied to the whole hospital.

Process Re-engineering and the SDU Concept

The essence of the changes were described by a leading clinician as "a move from separate vertical hierarchies for doctors, nurses and managers toward a more horizontally-orientated multi-disciplinary team culture". The main elements were: describing hospital work in process terms; producing an organizational structure enabling management of those processes and related resources; and developing IS supportive of the new arrangements. Using process analysis, and an incremental bottom-up approach, nearly 70 Service Delivery Units (SDUs) or service areas were identified. An example of an SDU is shown in Fig. 3. Though no rigid model was developed, there are several typical aspects of an SDU:

● It became responsible for delivering a defined set of services to patients or other SDUs, and consumed resources that it owned or bought in from other units.
● A senior clinician and nursing manager would lead an SDU and develop and manage its service plan.
● It became responsible for delivering services and managing its own resources.

SDUs were grouped into Service Centres (SC) of related medical specialities or support services, each with, typically, a clinical consultant chairperson

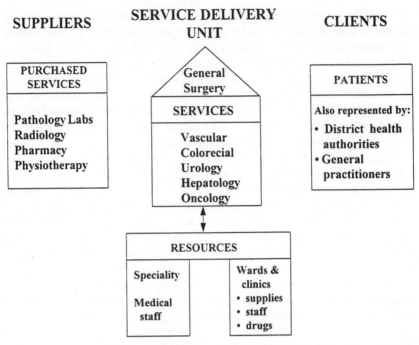

FIG. 3.   Example of a service delivery unit.

and full-time service manager. These would be responsible for interfacing with senior hospital management. SC chairpeople would meet senior management monthly as the hospital strategy and policy board, SC managers and senior management fortnightly as the hospital operational board. Essentially, the approach pushed down responsibility and accountability to the SDU level, and gave professional staff, such as clinicians and senior nursing staff, critical roles in management.

Information and IS would provide vital underpining to the new organizational arrangements. In the period under study existing IT-based systems were widely adjudged inadequate even for previous ways of working. An Information Strategy Steering Committee (ISSC) of senior managers, clinicians, and IT specialists involved a wide range of hospital staff in a number of task groups for developing ways forward. Early on it was commonly recognized that not only eliciting the information requirements but also developing and implementing the information systems needed would have to be incremental and highly participative processes. Some reasons for this are suggested by the following comment by an IT consultant:

> We're finding the hospital a very complex place in which to develop information systems. We're taking an evolutionary approach, and supporting the process changes. Even in low level jobs, there are major differences in the

way one secretary does the same job to another one. The technical problems are small; it's defining what's needed and getting the agreement and buy-in that's taking the time.

Moreover, systems had to be developed to meet not just clinician needs but also to underpin SDU operations, budgeting, and management, together with meeting higher-level hospital requirements. A range of interest groups pulled in several different directions at once, not least clinicians with considerable power. According to one senior clinician:

> The hospital will demand data from me in my management role, but if they insist on a data collection through a system unfriendly to us at the operational end—in how we do our jobs—then they will get data but it will not be accurate. These sorts of issues mean that we [doctors] need to be fully involved in the management of implementation.

Clearly, it was not just the complexity of the environment and the difficulties in identifying information requirements that led to an evolutionary, bottom-up approach, but also the political dimensions inherent in the situation.

Extended Implementation 1992–95

Throughout 1991–92 a new hospital information system based on client server architecture and open systems was prototyped. Different SDUs would share the same data held on a patient data server, essentially a hospital-wide database of data collected mostly by the SDUs. The database would hold all details relating to patients treated at the hospital. This data could be used in different ways in a range of activities, including contract and case-mix management, financial management, SDU work, and for clinical support. Additionally SDUs would develop their "private" information needed exclusively to support their own activities. Both the common and "private" data would be available through new user-friendly clinical workstations; these would be linked to the patient data server, and also to each other where required.

By 1993 the new process-based structure was in place and working. On the whole, clinicians were positive about running their own service groups. Operationally the new arrangements were held to be more efficient, despite rising pressure, financial constraint, and unprecedented demand in terms of patient numbers. Forward planning had also become more accurate. Throughout 1993–95 the information systems were being rolled out slowly. Politically and culturally this approach was acknowledged as a wise one, for example the following comment from a nursing manager in Trauma Services:

> The way that the IT-systems are lagging behind is quite positive. In devolved management, unless you have got a team used to and wanting to work together

and take responsibility you can have all the IT systems you like but it's not going to work. This way we also are becoming much more clear about the systems and information we really need.

Even so, a number of respondents suggested that implementation plans were not being well communicated even to immediately affected stake-holders. Also many nurses still remained cautious to sceptical about the usefulness of information systems in their work. Additionally, in the more advanced implementations in the Critical Care SDUs, there were potential problems arising as a result of lack of experience within the SDUs of rolling out information systems. Funding issues were also being raised, in particular about getting enough terminals and operators for data entry, and getting sufficient IT support staff. There was also emerging a shortage of time and resources—human and financial—to support the IT/IS training required in each SDU. A senior clinician summarized the implementation problems:

> End-games are difficult in the NHS. Government or the Department of Health, for example, move the goal posts, staff move on, outside support in the form of consultants and software suppliers starts working then funding runs out. You also get political opposition, given the range of professional groups and stakeholders. In information systems there are many interests to look after. Not only must it be a patient-centred system that also produces management information; critically it needs to be a user-centred system as well.

CASE ANALYSIS AND DISCUSSION

In this section a comparative analysis of the cases is presented utilizing a five-factor framework (see Table 1). The analysis is then developed further through a comparison of the case study findings against those from parallel studies by the authors and others on issues and risks in major BPR and IT projects.

Only in the case of National Vulcan could the BPR programme be con-sidered largely complete as at mid-1995. At the John Radcliffe Hospital (JRH) senior management had opted for a longer time span for completion. In itself this could become a significant risk factor. Survey respondents and commentators typically stress the need for rapid completion of core process re-engineering, preferably within 12 months. Otherwise loss of focus and momentum occur coupled with loss of enthusiasm and commitment from top management (Hammer & Stanton, 1995; Heygate, 1993; Willcocks, 1995a). Our own survey of completed BPR programmes found core process re-engineering averaging 11.4 months. However, the re-engineering activity tended to be smaller in scale than in the two cases. The scale of activity in the cases presented in itself a further risk element and also contributed to risk by elongating time-scales.

TABLE 1
Five-factor Analysis of Two Strategic BPR Projects

	National Vulcan (insurance)	John Radcliffe (health care)
Pressure to act	Poor financial performance, loss of major customer. New chief executive appointed by holding company.	Government imposed reforms. Development of internal health care market. Pressure to measure and improve performance. Budgetary constraints.
Locus of support	Senior management team and IT director. Promotion into project roles of those supporting changes.	Grown over time, rolled out through management, clinical, and nursing groups in each SDU. Senior clinicians supported process of change.
Change levers	Wide use of consultants/suppliers. IT identified as key enabler. Sustained focus on radical change throughout the company.	Careful use of external consultants. Methods not imposed. Facilitation of mutual incremental learning. Need to respond to external pressures.
Themes	"The valuable difference"; 24-hour turnaround for customer service; best quality, lowest cost provider.	Improved measurement and control. Devolved responsibility. Empowerment of service staff. IS in a support role.
Approach	Top down. Identify key processes. 3 project teams operate simultaneously. 9-month time constraint. Continuous open communication about "the new world". Business managers in control of projects.	Bottom up. Get clinicians involved. Use of consultants to develop incremental learning. Representative steering committees. Service delivery staff responsible for changes.
Outcome	Return to profit within two years. 25% reduction in job numbers. £6.2m IT development spend. Negligible customer complaints. HO–branch tensions. Skills issues. Reduced management layers.	Painstaking, evolutionary roll-out across Service Delivery Units within severe budgetary and resource constraints.

In the case of NV, respondents were generally agreed that BPR had been, in business terms, largely successful. In the JRH case respondents generally felt that in a changing NHS environment the hospital was a complex organization in which to attempt re-engineering, that steady progress had been made, but that the activity was at least two difficult years from its endpoint.

National Vulcan

In National Vulcan, BPR was initially driven by the declining competitive position manifested in poor financial performance. A new chief executive signalled change, and forcefully communicated a sense of crisis and urgency throughout the BPR programme. Part of the rhetoric of change created by senior management included the "valuable difference", "24-hour turnaround", and "best for less" concepts. These were used to focus daily attention and to underpin and communicate the longer-term vision of the re-engineered company. A top-down approach saw a small group of senior managers together with three business-led project teams push through IT systems development and implementation, aided by consultants, newly hired systems staff, and suppliers. The high age profile of the existing labour force made early retirement a major option to ease 25% reductions in job numbers enabled by large-scale application of new technologies. The setting of tight time-scales, for example nine months for completion of all the major systems development, appeared to focus effort and attention, including that of senior management.

The significant factors enabling senior management to achieve their re-engineering objectives would seem to include: the ability of the senior executives to create what was called a "burning platform" equating radical change with business survival; the poor state the company was in made dramatic improvements more easy to achieve; the ability to deliver workable technological solutions quickly to underpin the re-engineered processes; and continuous, focused senior management drive and attention. A further set of factors would appear significant, namely clear key processes, and an identifiable strategic business unit with clear objectives and relatively straightforward, easily-monitored performance criteria, including its financial results. Several parallel studies support the finding that radical re-engineering appears easier to achieve in such organizations (Harvey, 1995; Willcocks, 1995a). An interesting contrast is the more problematic re-engineering experienced in the complex JRH environment (70 SDUs identified), and also in a further case we have researched—that of the Columbus re-engineering project at the The Royal Bank of Scotland. In this case we found a strong correlation between implementation difficulties and the greater complexity and larger size of the organization (Currie & Willcocks, in press).

John Radcliffe Hospital

In the JRH case there was also clear and demanding external pressure to act due to radical reforms imposed by Government. However, it was clear that little could be achieved unless the diverse professional and occupational groupings of which the hospital staff comprised actively supported change. The locus of support was throughout management, clinical, and nursing echelons, but this had to be grown over time through the incremental, participative approach adopted. BPR provided a mode of addressing fundamental and intractable problems that previous attempts had failed to resolve. The pilot studies enabled basic problems to be addressed, established workable alternatives, and also released the energy needed for change. The careful use of consultants also provided levers for change; methods were not imposed, but rather both BPR and IS consultants facilitated incremental learning both by themselves and key stakeholders. A strong point favouring the new BPR activity was that much had been learnt from past experiences in the organization about how *not* to introduce large-scale change and information systems into the organization.

What proved particularly important was the choice to relegate the development and implementation of IS to a support role, after processes had been re-engineered, and while the working arrangements were being refined. The political and human issues surrounding IS development and implementation were well understood, and explicitly managed through adoption of an incremental, prototyping, user-led approach, rolling out the information systems an SDU at a time and carefully eliciting the different information requirements and IT/IS demands of each service unit. The approach adopted involved all salient stakeholders and, in terms of our earlier review of BPR, tended to be suitably multidisciplinary and holistic in its operationalization.

However, the case does demonstrate the long time period it requires to roll out an effective BPR programme within a large organization such as an acute NHS hospital. Though begun in 1991, the BPR activity in question was likely to continue into 1996, especially where delivering information systems to service units was concerned. This raises the question of whether there is a catch-22 in BPR: Effective large-scale BPR may take many years to implement, but can organizations wait that long for the effects to come through, and can energy, attention, and resources continue to be focused sufficiently to maintain momentum?

Risk in Major BPR Projects

The case findings can be related to earlier empirical work on profiling risks in major IT-enabled change projects (Willcocks & Griffiths, 1994; Willcocks & Margetts, 1994), where a central finding was that risk of failure correlated strongly to a drive into the technology resulting in a loss of focus on the business purpose to be achieved, and neglect of the fundamental organizational and behavioural changes implicated in, and fundamental to the delivery of espoused objectives. In both cases IT was utilized as a critical enabler of re-engineering. NV was interesting in reinventing itself technically, and gained advantage first (and ironically), from starting from a low technical base, and second, from carrying out the IT aspects quickly and in a prototyping fashion with mixed project teams. JRH sought to mitigate risk by pursuing a more evolutionary, high involvement path technically. This proved successful to 1995 but was placing a strain on limited financial and human resources, raising some doubts about the sustainability of the approach.

In earlier work, risk of failure in major IT-enabled projects was also related to factors relating to history, external and internal contexts, content, and process of change.

History. The record of previous IT disappointments in the two cases did cause new ways of working on IT projects. In NV the lack of relevant IT experience meant greater emphasis on organizational learning and education/training in systems development. Both also bought in technical expertise to mitigate risk but, of the two organizations, NV seemed to rely more heavily on this approach, partly because it had more complex technical issues on a larger scale.

External Context. Environmental pressures for change became obvious to many of the workforce in both cases, and this mitigated to some extent tensions and problems during re-engineering activity. However, supplier problems could also create risks, as most clearly seen in the NV case where Wang and Ingres ran into financial/market problems, but as we found in the NV case and in the Columbus project at The Royal Bank of Scotland (Currie & Willcocks, in press), difficulties could also arise from newness of the technology and consequent skills shortages in the market.

Internal Context. In both organizations, radical re-engineering, by definition, meant wholesale change in structure, strategy, reward systems, skills, culture, management styles, and levels and types of teamwork. This inevitably implied the generation of major political and cultural issues which, in practice, represented the major risks in both cases.

Process. These issues prompted different responses. NV took a "big bang", open communication approach on a relatively short time-scale to push through changes. In JRH a more evolutionary approach was taken in recognition of the difficulties inherent in winning over an entrenched set of occupational and professional groups that made up the workforce. In a further strategic re-engineering project we have researched—at the Royal Bank of Scotland—the approach seemed less convincing to many respondents because it appeared to embody mixed messages: full staff involvement on the one hand, large job reductions and senior management "pushing through" changes on the other (Currie & Willcocks, in press).

Content. The greater radical content of change largely helps to explain the greater degree of risk prevalent in the Royal Bank of Scotland case. In looking at BPR and the related IT projects the major risk factors we have identified elsewhere in major change projects—size complexity, number of units involved, technical uncertainty (because of new technologies), and definitional uncertainty (lack of clarity on business requirements)—these factors in fact were all at their greatest in the Royal Bank of Scotland case.

It is noteworthy here that, correspondingly, the Columbus re-engineering project, up to the end of 1995, was experiencing a lot more difficulties than the two other projects under review here.

BPR and the Technological Imperative

In the NV and JRH cases, re-engineering core processes were to be heavily dependent on IT to deliver the anticipated dramatic performance improvements. In this respect they reflect in practice a central theme of most of the management literature. It is useful therefore to analyse further the contrasting ways in which technology was to be delivered to the two organizations.

In both cases business goals and the processes to be re-engineered were defined before IT requirements were arrived at. That avoided many of the problems associated with being too IT-led. NV's approach of fast systems development in time-constrained projects led by business managers achieved stretch objectives, and provided considerable organizational learning on IT, despite numerous mistakes being made and a range of problems with suppliers. The development and management of "low value" systems was outsourced, but this resulted in a lack of control over user demands and costly overfunctionality of systems. Subsequently, business analysis and consultancy aspects of these systems were brought back in house. BPR was enabled by a rapid build-up of skills through bringing in full-time staff and contractors organized into four teams. Intensive and ongoing training of user staff supported the widespread use of IT from a previously low technical base in NV. The company had an advantage over JRH in having few "legacy" systems/technical skills. This factor, allied with the development approach and high levels of staff development for IT, enabled fast application of client-server technologies.

In JRH there were relatively few technical problems once the information requirements had been defined. The evolutionary user-led approach was proving successful, if difficult to sustain. The major problems stemmed from finding time and resources for user training, and securing technical support once systems had been implemented in an SDU.

A useful contrast can be made with the Columbus project at the Royal Bank of Scotland. This project experienced the biggest difficulties technically because of the relative size and complexity of the technical projects, the "newness" of the technologies, lack of relevant technical experience within the bank, and the problems of interfacing legacy mainframes with, for example, client-server technologies (Currie & Willcocks, in press).

Human, Cultural, and Political Issues

In the two cases it is worth highlighting that all management respondents deeming BPR as relatively successful cited management of human resource, cultural, and political issues as playing the really key role in that success.

This finding is strikingly supported in our survey work. Here respondents identified the following as in the top five most persistent barriers to BPR programmes: (1) middle and line management resistance, (2) loss of commitment/non-enthusiastic support from the top, (3) prevailing culture and political structure, and (4) lower-level employee fear and resistance (Willcocks, 1995a).

In each case the new technical environment in itself had considerable political and human resource implications and impacts. In NV new technology could be equated with large reductions in job numbers for all but technical people. Even so, the large influx of technical staff and contractors signalled new working practices and types of contract, and that insurance was no longer a job for life. In NV the new technological environment symbolized the "new organization" in a positive sense, i.e. progress and investment, and so could be tied in with politics as the management of meaning (Pettigrew, 1985; Willcocks, Currie, & Mason, 1996). Simultaneously, it symbolized a threat to existing work practices, the distribution of power and resources, and "the way things were". This symbolic ambivalence had considerable political ramifications in NV, but much less so in JRH where the wider changes relating to introducing the internal market in health care had much greater symbolic significance.

More broadly, it could be seen that senior managers in each organization chose specific strategies for working through the political, cultural, and human resource aspects of radical change. In NV it was specifically top down with change pushed through by constant senior management pressure and attention. By way of contrast, in the Royal Bank of Scotland—a larger organization with much more extensive change envisaged—we found that senior management had to lever change through lower levels of management, project management, and widespread use of contractors. This inevitably dissipated focus. Moreover the senior management's "New Bank" vision of the future represented a significant departure from traditional banking. In its human resources implications, it could be perceived as threatening interests and change at all levels (Currie & Willcocks, in press). Not surprisingly, we found more evidence of emergent protectionist strategies amongst the workforce in the Royal Bank of Scotland than in NV, while in JRH the explicit political strategy of those managing the BPR activity was to go with the existing culture and ways of working in order to win over the entrenched interest groups without whom the re-engineering could not go ahead. Moreover, re-engineering at JRH did not have the large job losses so explicitly associated with radical change in the other two cases. Also, although departments and processes were being reconstituted at JRH as at NV, in the hospital there was less breakdown of the traditional skills base, and a lesser degree of retraining and multiskilling inherent in the changes.

CONCLUSION

Of the two cases, the National Vulcan experience is perhaps the most typical of radical re-engineering as put forward by Hammer & Champy (1993). We have pointed out elsewhere (Grint, Case, & Willcocks, 1995), as has Davenport (1993a), the contradiction represented in the violence inherent in their approach to human resource issues against their stress on the vital role people play in the re-engineered world of empowerment, teamwork, achievement culture, and devolved responsibility. The stress on imposing change quickly, and rooting out resistance, can be contrasted with one of the top 10 ways of failing at re-engineering—"ignore the concerns of your people" (Hammer & Stanton, 1995). At National Vulcan, the human resource and political problems inherent in radical engineering were ameliorated by the ease with which job reductions could be made through early retirement and voluntary redundancy, through constant top management attention to the political and human resource issues, because of an open communications policy, and due to the dramatic improvements that could be made from the low start point of the organization in performance terms.

It was also clear that radical re-engineering on the Hammer and Champy (1993) model was more possible in a definable business unit like NV with relatively simple structures, clear objectives and where performance and improvement is easily measured. These characteristics were not so prevalent in the hospital case, nor indeed in the Royal Bank of Scotland case that we have analysed in detail elsewhere (see Currie & Willcocks, in press). It is significant that the JRH did not attempt radical re-engineering along Hammer and Champy lines, while at the Royal Bank of Scotland organizational complexity and scale frequently pushed re-engineering activity into other directions. In particular the methodological holism central to radical re-engineering seemed difficult to deliver in the Royal Bank of Scotland Columbus project, and also the alignment between strategy and implementation became more distorted in that case than in NV and JRH.

The cases also reveal that the notion that senior managers can simply begin process innovation anew starting from a blank sheet of paper is somewhat unrealistic, at least in most cases, particularly as traditional practices and procedures both influence and inhibit the re-engineering activity. More broadly, in both cases the human, cultural, and political issues pointed up the degree to which continuity as well as change needed to be considered as part of re-engineering activity. For example, even in the NV case the most valuable part of the organization—that was duly preserved—was the skill base of the inspection engineers. The case studies also reveal that Hammer and colleagues all too easily adopt a unitary, largely senior management perspective on the organization, and as a result relegate politics and the pursuit of other stakeholder perspectives and interests as aberrant behaviour characterized as "resistance to change". Human resources are treated largely in mechanistic terms, passive recipients (ironically) of senior management "empowerment". The notion of organizations as complex, socio-cultural institutions with histories is seen largely, and largely rhetorically, in negative terms. Radical re-engineering offers senior management the opportunity to forget the past and to dismiss any responsibility for dealing with its residues and consequences (Grint et al., 1995). The cases help to illustrate that complexities of organization, the importance of continuity as a basis for change, and the political and cultural difficulties radical re-engineering stores up for itself by taking the "don't automate, obliterate" route, are all too easily lost in the attractive rhetoric of transformation through simplification. In all these aspects, of course, radical re-engineering is revealed as essentially political. Artefacts, in the form of re-engineered processes underpinned by technology, are powerful means of achieving objectives. The cases reveal that pursuing such objectives and means will invariably generate a range of human political and cultural issues central, not marginal, to radical re-engineering.

In earlier research we found very few organizations pursuing the radical re-engineering route, and only 18% of organizations achieving what could be called "breakthrough" performances as a result of re-engineering (Willcocks, 1995a, 1995b). While the present cases reveal what radical re-engineering can entail, they may also serve to indicate why many of the organizations we surveyed seemed to adopt a more low-risk process improvement approach that in the long term could achieve substantial, even similar levels of performance gains. Finally, against Hammer and several other commentators, it remains a moot point, of course, whether in practice, on a case by case basis, every organization can be identified as the "burning platform" that makes radical re-engineering so (rhetorically) necessary, and possible.

REFERENCES

Bartram, P. (1992). *Business reengineering: The use of process redesign and IT to transform corporate performance*. London: Business Intelligence.

Belmonte, R., & Murray, R. (1993). Getting ready for strategic change: Surviving business process redesign. *Information Systems Management, Summer*, 23–29.

Buday, R. (1992). Forging a new culture at Capital Holding's Direct Response Group. *Insights Quarterly, 4*, 38–49.

Currie, W. (1994). The strategic management of large scale IT projects in the financial services sector. *New Technology Work and Employment, 9*(1), 19–29.

Currie, W. (1995). *Management strategy for IT: An international perspective*. London: Pitman Publishing.

Currie, W., & Seddon, J. (1995, September). *Reengineering and process innovation at a UK bank: A case study on the development of a branch banking system.* Paper presented at the British Academy of Management Conference.

Currie, W., & Willcocks, L. (in press). The new branch Columbus project at Royal Bank of Scotland: The implementation of large-scale business process reengineering. *Journal of Strategic Information Systems.*

Davenport, H. (1993a). Book review of *Reengineering the corporation. Sloan Management Review, Fall*, 103–104.

Davenport, H. (1993b). *Process innovation: Reengineering work through information technology.* Boston, Mass.: Harvard Business Press.

Davenport, T., & Stoddard, D. (1994). Reengineering: Business change of mythic proportions? *MIS Quarterly, 18*(2), 121–127.

Earl, M., & Khan, B. (1994). How new is business process redesign? *European Management Journal, 12*(1), 20–30.

Galliers, R. (1994, April). *Information technology and organizational change: Where does BPR fit in?* Paper presented at the conference on Information Technology and Organisational Change: The Changing Role of IT and Business, Nijenrode University, Breukelen, The Netherlands.

Grint, K. (1993). *Reengineering history: An analysis of business process reengineering* (Management Research Paper 93/20). Oxford, UK: Templeton College.

Grint, K., Case, P., & Willcocks, L. (1995, December). *Business process reengineering: The politics and technology of forgetting.* Paper presented at the IFIP WG 8.2 Conference on Information Technology and Changes in Organizational Work, University of Cambridge, UK.

Grint, K., & Willcocks, L. (1995). Business process reengineering in theory and practice: Business paradise regained? *New Technology Work and Employment, 10*(2), 99–109.

Hall, G., Rosenthal, J., & Wade, J. (1993). How to make reengineering really work. *Harvard Business Review, November–December*, 119–131.

Hammer, M., & Champy, J. (1993). *Reengineering the corporation: A manifesto for business revolution.* London: Nicholas Brealey Publishing.

Hammer, M., & Stanton, S. (1994, October 5). No need for excuses. *Financial Times*, p. 20.

Hammer, M., & Stanton, S. (1995). *The reengineering revolution.* New York: Harper Collins.

Harvey, D. (1995). *Reengineering: The critical success factors.* London: Business Intelligence.

Heygate, R. (1993). Immoderate redesign. *The McKinsey Quarterly, 1*, 73–87.

Johannsson, H., McHugh, P., Pendlebury, A., & Wheeler, W. (1993). *Business process reengineering: Breakpoint strategies for market dominance.* Chichester, UK: John Wiley.

Klein, M. (1994). Reengineering methodologies and tools. *Information Systems Management, Spring*, 31–35.

Moad, J. (1993, August 1). Does reengineering really work? *Datamation*, pp. 22–28.

Morris, D., & Brandon, J. (1993). *Reengineering your business.* London: McGraw-Hill.

O'Hara, M., & Watson, R. (1995). Automation, business process reengineering and client server technology: A three stage model of organizational change. In V. Grover & W. Kettinger (Eds.), *Business process change: Reengineering concepts, methods and technologies.* Harrisburg, Penn.: Idea Group Publishing.

Pettigrew, A. (1985). *The awakening giant: Continuity and change at ICI.* Oxford: Blackwell.

Pettigrew, A., Ferlie, E., & McKee, L. (1992). *Shaping strategic change.* London: Sage.

Pettigrew, A., & Whipp, R. (1991). *Managing change for competitive success.* Oxford: Blackwell.

Smith, G., & Willcocks, L. (1995). Business process reengineering, politics and management: From methodologies to processes. In V. Grover & W. Kettinger (Eds.), *Business process change: Reengineering concepts, methods and technologies.* Harrisburg, Penn.: Idea Group Publishing.

Stringer, J. (1992). Risks in large projects. In M. Mortimer (Ed.), *Operational research tutorial papers*. London: Operational Research Society.

Walsham, G. (1993). *Interpreting information systems in organizations*. Chichester, UK: Wiley.

Walton, R. (1989). *Up and running*. Boston, Mass.: Harvard Business Press.

Watson, G. (1995). *Business systems engineering*. New York: Wiley.

Willcocks, L. (1995a). A survey of current BPR practice. In D. Harvey, M. Maletz, & L. Willcocks (Eds.), *Reengineering: The critical success factors*. London: Business Intelligence.

Willcocks, L. (1995b, July). *False promise or delivering the goods? Recent findings on the economics and impact of business process reengineering*. Paper presented at the Second European Conference on IT Evaluation, Henley Management College, Henley, UK.

Willcocks, L. (Ed.). (1996). *Investing in information systems: Evaluation and management*. London: Chapman & Hall.

Willcocks, L., Currie, W., & Mason, D. (1996). *Information systems at work: People, politics and technology*. Maidenhead, UK: McGraw-Hill.

Willcocks, L., & Griffiths, C. (1994). Predicting the risk of failure in major information technology projects. *Technological Forecasting and Social Change, 47*(2), 205–228.

Willcocks, L., & Margetts, H. (1994). Risk and information systems: Developing the analysis. In L. Willcocks (Ed.), *Information management: Evaluation of information systems investments*. London: Chapman & Hall.

EUROPEAN JOURNAL OF WORK AND ORGANIZATIONAL PSYCHOLOGY, 1996, 5 (3), 351–375

Technological and Organizational Innovation: A Dilemma of Fundamental Change and Participation

Jaap J. Boonstra

Organizational Studies, University of Amsterdam, Amsterdam, The Netherlands

Maurits J. Vink

SANT Management Consultancy, Amsterdam, The Netherlands

This article proposes sociotechnical system theory as a framework for analysing the relationship between technological and organizational innovation and as a tool for managing change as a process of organizational learning. The article focuses on the barriers to change and the way in which the dilemma between expert design and participatory development is approached. The technological and organizational innovation in an automated clearing house for payment transactions has been used as an example. The longitudinal case research focuses on the dynamics of change and illustrates the importance of learning processes during the innovation to realize flexibility and innovative capacity within the organization. The article concludes that sociotechnical system theory provides a basis of knowledge for redesigning organizations as well as developing organizations by learning processes. It indicates six barriers to technological and organizational innovation and offers a perspective on how to integrate design strategies with a participative learning strategy for fundamental change.

INTRODUCTION

An understanding of the development and implementation of technological and organizational innovations is crucial, given the importance of these innovations to the improvement of labour and work processes in organizations. The development and introduction of new information technologies are directly related to changes in business strategy, the flow of information, and the design of business processes. Technological development also creates the potential for new choices in work organization and the quality of working life (Child & Loveridge, 1990; Walton, 1988).

Influenced by technological innovations and higher market demands, organizations strive to enhance their flexibility and ability to innovate and to

Requests for reprints should be addressed to J.J. Boonstra, Organizational Studies, University of Amsterdam, O.Z. Achterburgwal 237, 1012 DL Amsterdam, The Netherlands.

increase their learning capacities. The traditional organizational paradigm of maximal division of labour is increasingly abandoned. Attempts are made to break with the functional structuring of organizations by redesigning business processes on the basis of customers or product flows. Within these flows, self-managing teams are formed. These teams integrate operational tasks with planning, support, and control activities. The teams are to a certain extent autonomous and are expected to improve the execution of assignments while learning (Cherns, 1987; Herbst, 1976).

The realization of technological and organizational innovation is a complex change process and many organizations do not attain the desired outcomes. A possible explanation for these failures can be found in the approach of the change process. Fundamental organizational change tries to create flexible organizations with a high innovative potential, but at the same time most of our organizations lack the learning capacities that are needed for innovation. So, what are the barriers to complete transformation of business and how can traditional organizations learn to become learning and innovative organizations?

A dilemma is that an expert design approach permits a far-reaching break through innovation but it neglects the development of learning capacities, whereas a participatory development approach gives way to learning but the drawback is that it allows participants to fall back to conventional and fragmental solutions in their thoughts and deeds, while innovative and completely new ideas are needed.

This article examines the barriers to technological and organizational innovation and explores the tension between expert design and participative development. In the first section, the relation between technological and organizational innovation will be conceptualized in a system theory of organizations. It will also consider the way in which fundamental change is achieved by business process redesign (BPR) and sociotechnical system theory (STST). The second section presents the results of an in-depth longitudinal case study. The relations between business strategy, information technology, work organization, and the quality of working life will be made clear. The focus of the study is to examine the barriers to change and the way in which the dilemma between expert design and participatory development is approached. In the third section we present some lessons for realizing technological and organizational innovation.

THEORETICAL FRAMEWORK

System Theory of Organizations

For technological and organizational innovation and the integration of change to take place, some unifying framework is needed to guide the process. The open sociotechnical systems theory offers such a framework.

Organizations are viewed as open systems. The production process takes place within socio-economic exchange networks between the organization and its environment. Economic, technological, and social developments form a complex of more or less structured situations that affect the organization and influence its functioning (Emery & Trist, 1965). Interactions take place between the organization and stakeholders within the transactional environment (Ansoff, 1985; Freeman, 1984). In order to survive, an organization has to respond adequately to changes in the environment and the relations with stakeholders. The environment of many organizations is becoming more complex and changes occur at an ever increasing pace, compelling organizations to develop a more flexible and innovative work organization.

The sociotechnical perspective considers every organization to be made up of a social and a technological aspect-system. People working together in an organizational context (the social system) are using information systems, tools, techniques, and knowledge (the technical system) to produce a service or product valued by the environment (the environmental system) (Emery, 1959; Pasmore, 1988; Trist, 1982). The social and technological aspect-systems interact continuously and are inclined towards a dynamic equilibrium in relation to the environment of the organization. Change in one aspect-system directly affects its relation to other aspect-systems (Pava, 1986). The ability of each of the systems to adjust means that the organization forms a flexible system capable of adjusting to environmental changes.

The sociotechnical system theory provides a useful framework for assessing the system-wide implications of information technologies (Shani & Sena, 1994). Compatibility between the technical and environment aspect-systems requires that new information technologies are effective in meeting the needs of the stakeholders. Introducing new technology inevitably requires a redefinition of the relationship between the organization and the environment through adjustment to business strategy. Compatibility between technical and social aspect-systems implies that a balance must be struck between the new information technologies with the social aspect-system to accommodate the requirements of the new information technology (Clark & Staunton, 1989).

Technological and Organizational Innovation

The introduction of new information technology in organizations will involve the development of new ideas about technical and social processes and is related to business strategy and business processes. This perspective contrasts with technological determinism in which technology determines the social aspect-system and organizational choices cannot be made on how to relate the technological and social aspect-systems (Turner & Lawrence, 1965). Swan and Clark (1992) debate that cognitive processes and decision making are important in the process of innovation and the choices to be made. A question is how the existing organizational paradigm influences the decision-making process on technological and organizational innovation. Weick (1990) argues that people design technology and organizations in keeping with their perceptions and explanatory frameworks. This viewpoint is subscribed to by Child and Loveridge (1990). In a study on information technology in European services they concluded that the opportunities offered for organizational innovation by information technology appear to have been realized very frequently; only occasionally had substantial change in organizational design and tasks structure been introduced. This lack of novelty might be attributed to a delayed process of organizational learning in which existing perspectives continue to dominate. There seems to be a process of organizational conservatism that is shaped and bound by forces of a social and political nature in the sense that those involved have a concern to preserve organizational arrangements with which they are comfortable. Traditions that are long-established and have institutionalized into bureaucratic structures, and strong cultures as a means of ensuring predictability, support the prevailing systems of the division of labour.

Realizing strategic, technological, and organizational change is a difficult process and a lot of efforts fail to realize the objectives. Beer (1988) gives reasons why broad change programmes fail. First, programmes seem to be unidimensional and do not change the technical and social aspect system at the same time. In addition, programmes are seldom targeted at behaviour. Second, programmatic changes are often not connected to the most pressing problems experienced by employees. At best, the programmes are a response to a general diagnosis of business problems. This makes it difficult to learn from earlier experiences and to translate the general themes into action. Third, the programmes are often initiated and managed by top management and experts. This top-down and expert character makes it difficult for employees and line management to feel committed. Swan and Clark (1992) indicate that particular problems occur when employees have inadequate knowledge bases and have conflicting ideas about the chosen innovation. Knowledge and cognitions are important in the innovation process. Organizational as well as technological knowledge bases are important to decisions about technological innovation because its appropriation requires a blending of technical systems with organizational procedures and practice.

Design Perspective on Organizational Change

The term business process redesign (BPR) is often used when redesign of strategy, information technology, and organizational processes is concerned (Davenport, 1993; Hammer & Champy, 1993). In essence, BPR is a fundamental rearrangement of business processes enabling information technology to realize reduction of costs, increase of profitability, and enhancement of performance in quality, service, and speed.

The design philosophy of BPR concerns the radical redesign of business processes. Business processes are rearranged on a customer or product basis. In the customer- or product-oriented process design, process segments are placed in a natural sequence. Teams bear the responsibility for the execution of tasks within a segment and are held accountable for measurable results. Frequently, separate teams are formed for innovation, planning and preparation, and execution of tasks. The operational teams are confronted with an elaborately modelled and automated production method. In the application of redesign principles in the service sector, a distinction is often made between a front office for direct interaction with customers and a back office for administrative processing. In the front office the task is to inform the customer quickly and adequately. Information technology enables decision making while the customer is served. In the back office all activities suitable for automation are subsumed. The technological governance of the work process results in a situation in which people have little influence over their own actions and in which they face considerably increased expectations with respect to their work pace and output. Teams are expected to contribute to the enhancement of a more efficient production method.

The organization of the redesign process is primarily a task of the management. Top management contributes to the motivation for change and is responsible for the designation of goals and the allocation of means. Teams of line managers are responsible for the design of sub-processes. A steering committee of managers develop the strategy for the change process and co-ordinate the course of events. Consultants support the entire process with techniques and resources (Harrison & Pratt, 1993). In the design methodology a number of stages are distinguished. Teams of managers analyse business processes and circumscribe performance criteria for the redesign. With the consultant's assistance, a perspective is developed on the organization of business processes. The analyses of the teams are combined into a blueprint for the organization form, the appropriate technological architecture and information systems. The new organization form is implemented by the line management. Communication about the importance of the new design is seen as a success factor for change. Pilot projects and training programmes could illustrate the significance of change. Finally, team-based activities are built into the entire organization in order to replace conventional management methods (Guha, Kettinger, & Teng, 1993; Harrison & Pratt, 1993).

Development Perspective on Organizational Change

The development perspective on organizational change is based on sociotechnical experiences. The sociotechnique was initially preoccupied with the criteria for the design of tasks on an individual or group level. The purpose of this redesign was an improvement of organizational effectiveness, an improvement of the quality of work life, and the levelling of power. In the 1970s and 1980s, the sociotechnical design principles were further developed into an integral redesign of organizations. In this integral redesign, attention is paid to the relation between corporate strategy, organizational form, the nature of the transformation process, the technology, and labour.

The central design principle of the contemporary sociotechnique can be summarized as the formation of complex tasks within simple structures, instead of the performance of simple tasks within complex structures. What is central is the shift from the maximal division of work in classically structured organizations to the minimal division of work as the leading principle of design for flexible and modern organizations. According to sociotechnical views, the team is the smallest unit of organizing. In the organization, groups are always interdependent. It would benefit the flexibility, the effectiveness, and the quality of work life, if groups can regulate their own tasks, can shape their own work organization, have a high measure of control and the ability to solve problems independently (Ashby, 1969; Cherns, 1987; Susman, 1976).

Management of the change process rests on experience in the practice of the classical organization development and is theoretically founded on theories of group dynamics, learning processes, process intervention, and systemic change (Argyris, 1990; Beer & Walton, 1987; Schein, 1969). Practical experience has led to the conclusion that insufficient results are achieved with the sociotechnical designs when a fundamental change process is based exclusively on the sociotechnical design principles. Van Beinum (1990) states that the change process will inevitably result in some form of "social engineering" when organizational redesign is shaped by external experts who, solely on the basis of a sociotechnical system analysis, prescribe how the new organization must be shaped. The members of the organization are then insufficiently involved in fundamental decisions and little opportunity is left for organizational learning and the incorporation and acceptance of the change process. The designing of organizations which is characterized by autonomy, self-regulation, and participation can, according to Van Beinum, only genuinely take place when all members are actively involved in the shaping of their own work situation and are allowed to experience a learning process during the change process that enhances their understanding of their own situation. A participative approach usually employs search conferences, group discussions, workshops, and the experience gained through team-based work to redesign the work organization (Mohrman & Cummings, 1989).

The Dilemma of Technological and Organizational Innovation

In the design perspective the emphasis lies on the application of new technology and the designing of a new organization. The design starts with the designation of abstract objectives. Particular attention is paid to the desired output of the organization, the formal transformation process, and the related information process. The change process is singular and linear, and the number of alternatives is restricted. If the new organization is implemented and a stable final situation is attained, the change process has been concluded. Changes are often initiated, co-ordinated, and controlled by the top of the organization. The decision-making process is highly structured and formalized. There is hardly any opportunity for a discussion of possible differences in opinion. The approach is normally supported by consultants who, as experts, primarily focus on the design of the new information technology and work organization. A problem with the design approach is that it hardly contributes to the enhancement of the ability to change on lower levels in the organization. Cultural and political aspects are easily left outside of consideration. There is a great danger that collective norms and values will not develop, power structures are not influenced, and that, therefore, fundamental change cannot be achieved.

In the development approach, organizational problems and shortcomings are analysed first. The organization's ability to change is enhanced by involving members of the organization in the problem analysis. During the process, attention is given to the organization's culture and capability of the people to solve problems. The decision-making process concentrates on attaining shared objectives by consultation and negotiation. There is a phased and progressive change in which ideas from the basis of the organization play an important role. The change process is characterized by rough planning. Members of the organization are involved in all phases of the process. Participation is very possible, because the starting-point is the existing organization, objectives are established gradually, and deliberation and adjustment are facilitated. By participation of all organizational members, an enhancement of the self-learning ability of all members is attempted. A problem with the development approach is that it is difficult to achieve fundamental changes. Because of the existing social and political nature, the grounded values, norms and traditions, and the existing bureaucratic structures, organizational conservatism supporting the prevailing systems of the division of labour and hindering fundamental organizational change can exist.

From an interventionist perspective, two important questions are raised: (1) What are the barriers to technological and organizational innovation? (2) What are the possibilities of broadening the perspectives of the participants in the decision-making process and overcoming organizational conservatism and simultaneously developing learning capacities?

RESEARCH SITE AND METHODOLOGY

Action research is a method to study dynamic processes and actions that are temporally interconnected and embedded in context. The research is aimed at developing descriptive accounts and explanations through looking at patterns of events to gain knowledge of problems and the solving of problems in social reality (Argyris, 1983).

The research reported in this section sought to address the dynamics of change over a three-year period in a single company faced with the demands of becoming more flexible and integrating strategic, technological, and organizational innovation. The research is based on real-time longitudinal analyses of the change process and a retrospective analysis of the collected data and the acquired experiences and knowledge. The second author of the study served as a consultant in a team of internal and external employees that facilitated the change process. The first author facilitated the action research process during the study. Data collection involved ongoing semi-structured interviews, the keeping of a diary, questionnaires, conferences, workshops, and quarterly process evaluations.

The research has been conducted in the BankGiroCentrale (BGC), an automated clearing house for payment transactions for the commercial banks in the Netherlands. The product of the BGC is operation services of pre-arranged batch payment items submitted on magnetic tape, diskettes, computer-cartridges, cheques, payment documents, and conversion forms. The BGC is also providing data-networks for cash dispensers, point-of-sale terminals, and telegiro. In addition, BGC is processing and exchanging information about payment transactions between banks and is supporting the standardization and the risk management in information technology for payment transactions. The BGC has two processing centres in the Netherlands and 800 people are employed by the organization.

A CASE OF FUNDAMENTAL CHANGE

BGC as an Open System

The market of payment transactions has become rather turbulent during the last years. The costs of payment transactions has to be reduced under the influence of the demands of the commercial banks and their customers. New forms of payment by credit card, debit card, or data communication require low transaction costs, reliable operation, high performance, and security. Deregulation of the financial services by government offers possibilities for merging bank activities with insurance. The pursuit of a European economic and monetary market by the European Commission influences the scaling of the financial market and an increase of international activities and collaboration by banks and insurance companies. Competition between financial conglomerates is rising. This leads to very strong stake-holders that put higher demands on costs and the quality of services that is offered by the BGC. Banks make high demands on swift and timely processing of payments and settlement of payments between banks. Service levels and customer satisfaction are becoming more and more important.

The availability of swifter and better mainframe computers, the developments in information technology and the application of data communication have resulted in significant shifts in the different types of payment order. Transactions are more frequently presented on cartidges, tapes, and data communication than via paper. These shifts require adaptations in work organization and job qualifications. During the past few years, technological developments have generated all sorts of new services and products, such as cash dispensers, point-of-sale terminals, the development of the chip card, and the possibility of giving payment orders via interactive television. This demands an innovative capacity from an organization.

For the management of the BGC, the analysis of the environment formed the basis for a new business strategy. The environment and the changing market demands from the BGC further cost reduction, improvements in quality and customer service, a flexible attitude towards market developments, and an innovative ability to make optimal use of new information technology. The business strategy results in three projects: (1) the development of a new automated payment system including the renewal of system architecture and the technological infrastructure; (2) the realization of a new technological and logistic infrastructure for high-speed imaging of payment documents; (3) the re-engineering of the business processes and the reorganization of the company into an effective and efficient organization that is compatible with the new information technology.

BGC as a Sociotechnical System

Information technology is essential for the functioning of the BGC. All payment orders are processed by means of automated systems. The information on the production is recorded in automated data files or on microfilm. All the BGC products are highly automated. Administrative organization and procedures are important in order to keep track of the transformation process and to reduce susceptibility to fraud. The existing information systems no longer met requirements because of the high cost of maintenance and the limited possibilities of adaptation. Furthermore, the system was insufficiently capable of coping with the growth in financial traffic and it no longer met the requirements of swift and reliable processing. The new information systems were to be flexible and easily maintained. In the new system, a distinction is made between technical management of the hardware control systems and functional management of the application systems.

To realize compatibility between the new technological aspect-system and the social aspect system, the top management installed task groups of line managers to study the effects of the new technology on the organizational structure. This gradually revealed that the line managers were unable fully to consider the operational processes. The task groups reached a deadlock in discussions on the adjustment of the boundaries between the existing departments. There proved to be an organizational conservatism in which line managers proceed from the present division of labour and try to protect their own position within the organization. At the same time, employees are worried about the effect of the technological innovation on the quality of working life. A committee for the quality of working life discussed the perils of technological determinism and the possible negative consequences of the new technology with the top management.

The top management, confronted with the limited capacity to change of the line management and the uncertainty of the employees, asked for assistance from consultants in managing the technological and the organizational innovation.

Facilitating the Change Process

The formulated strategic policy induced the innovation of the technical aspect-system. The strategic policy had been limitedly communicated within the organization and only a few organization members had been involved in the technological innovations. So far, little attention had been paid to the social aspect-system. The advisers suggested a clarification of organizational strategy and a formulation of the points of departure for the changing technological and social aspect-system. A conference model was chosen to elaborate the points of departure (Axelrod, 1992; Weisbord, 1992).

In the work conferences, the top management presented the analysis of the environment and market changes and discussed the strategic goals with the line management and the employees. Three work conferences were held, with about 40 participants per conference. The participants were a cross-section of the organization. Besides discussions on the strategic objectives and the development of information technology, pressure points within the existing organization were analysed and an inventory was made of suggestions for improvement. Additionally, success factors for change were charted. The outcome of the work conferences was the basis of the points of departure for the renewal of the technological and social system and of the way in which the change process was to be dealt with. The points of departure were presented during group meetings and discussed with all employees. During these meetings the feasibility of the change was specifically discussed.

In order to further facilitate the change process, a task force of employees and external advisers was formed. The task of this group was to gather information on pressure points within the organization and to organize work meetings to develop proposals for the new set-up of the organizational processes and to formulate ideas for an appropriate form of organization. The task force consisted of employees who collectively had a clear image of the work processes in the different departments and who were considered capable of guiding group discussions on the future work organization. Top management and the work council were both involved in the change process by means of regular meetings and workshops. Line management was involved in work conferences. Employees were involved in questionnaires and group discussions to diagnose problems in the social aspect-system and in workshops to suggest ideas for problem solving and to develop new designs for business processes, information technology, and work organization.

Problem Diagnosis in the Social System

The points of departure and the reactions to them formed the basis on which a specific form of diagnosis was developed for each unit. Three units are to be distinguished within the production process. (1) *Operations* dealt with the processing of payment traffic. About 450 people, spread over two branches, were active in this unit. The unit had been organized in a linear structure with small processing steps divided over many departments. The processing was to be distinguished into: (a) receipt and unpacking and sorting of tapes, diskettes, and cartridges, (b) control of payment information, (c) input of data, (d) correction and recoding of data, (e) authorization and automated processing, and (f) production and supply of output. Separate service departments in Operations supplied telephonic and written information on the processing. (2) *Commercial Affairs* dealt with the account management of clients and with the product management of payment products. About 50 people were active in this unit. The department also developed specific automated applications for individual banks. (3) *Computer and Network Services* dealt with the technical support of the operations, in particular. About 250 people were active in this unit. The unit supplied computer and network facilities for the processing and took care of the daily control of the applications needed for the processing. Additionally, the unit developed new information systems in accordance with the wishes of the commercial unit.

The diagnosis consisted of interviews, specific questionnaires for all the employees and group discussions to verify and discuss the results of the questionnaire. The questionnaire included such items as contacts with customers, exchange of information and compatibility among departments, pressure points in the work, style of leadership, quality of working life, and barriers to fundamental change. The diagnosis provides a sharp picture of the problems within the various units.

Operations was characterized by a far-reaching division of labour. The number of functional contacts between the departments was very high and a great deal of co-ordination of different tasks is required in order to have the work process run smoothly. The exchange of information and the task co-ordination took a lot of time, proceeded with difficulty, and caused a great deal of attuning problems and mistakes in the operations. The quality of working life was rather low owing to limited tasks with little responsibility. Employees were given limited information on the achievement of results. Owing to their dependence on others they had few opportunities to solve the problems encountered in their own work. There was a very limited learning potential.

Commercial Affairs was differentiated in account managers, product managers, and customer services. Account managers as well as product managers visited customers but the co-ordination between the two departments was very problematic. The customers' questions about operations were answered by customer services as well as by the service desk from operations. The result was that clients did not know which department to turn to and that they were often referred from one department to another. No systematic survey was kept of the problems, questions, and wishes of the clients. Relations between Commercial Affairs and Operations was problematic because Commercial Affairs made promises to clients that Operations was unable to fulfil.

Computer and Network Services consisted of about 20 departments. Half of them dealt with day-to-day hardware operations and the operating of the information systems for the transactions in the unit operations. The activities of this service unit and the unit operations needed a lot of co-ordination. This co-ordination often proceeded with difficulty owing to distances between locations and differences in time between the detection of problems in the execution of the payment traffic and the control of this traffic by means of automated systems. The departments dealing with the development of systems were all responsible for a separate phase within the system development or for a specific technological subject. For the greater part, the co-ordination of these activities within the unit proceeded with difficulty.

The outcomes of the diagnosis have been widely presented within the organization. For this purpose, general information sessions were organized, as well as presentations to smaller groups. The presentations were given by the management. This way they emphasized that the pressure points that had been indicated in the diagnosis by the employees were taken seriously. The presentations were accompanied by written material in which the outlines of the outcomes had been listed systematically. During these presentations, the employees and the managers had the opportunity to respond to the outcomes and, if neccessary, to indicate gaps or mistakes. During the presentations it was also indicated which themes were to be further elaborated. The management had determined these themes on the basis of the outcomes of the diagnosis, in consultation with the heads of the department.

The diagnosis revealed that the high degree of task differentiation within the organization resulted in pressure points in the exchange of information, in the effectiveness of working by making projects, and in customer service. Task differentiation within the business processes resulted in a strong inter-dependence between departments and groups, which reduced the decisive-ness and efficiency of the organization; moreover, it put a heavy burden on communication and co-ordination. The task division also contributed to the fact that responsibilities were not assigned unambiguously. This limited the swiftness of reaction in case of changing circumstances or problems. The division of tasks also resulted in a limited quality of labour. If the present social aspect-system were to be taken as a starting point for further auto-mation, there is a risk that the deficiencies within this system would be embedded in the technology and that the opportunities for innovation of the entire organizational system would not be realized. Simultaneous innovation of the technical and social aspect-system was indicated in order to realize the strategic objectives and to meet the demands made on the organization by the environment.

Barriers to Change

One of the most important reasons why change programmes fail is that they do not deal with fundamental barriers to the development and implementa-tion of organizational and technological innovation (Beer, Eisenstat, & Spector, 1990). Therefore, three questions about the failures of change were included in the questionnaire. (1) Why were change programmes not successful in the past? (2) What are the barriers to the realization of the innovation as presented in the points of departure? (3) What is needed to solve the problems of this organization? The open questions were answered in writing by more than 60% of all employees. A content analysis of the answers was made by the task force and feedback was given to all the organizational members.

The answers revealed three significant reasons why change programmes had not been successful in the past: (1) because the employees had not been sufficiently informed; (2) because employees had not been involved in the changes; (3) because the changes had not been carried through on account of their possible consequences for the managers. Five significant barriers that may hinder the process were mentioned: (1) the quality of leadership and an autocratic style of management; (2) an ineffective top team and inadequate management skills in a bureaucratic structure with an overload of hierarchical levels; (3) the existing boundaries between the departments and the ensuing "realms", in combination with insufficient co-operation between the departments; (4) poor vertical communication and unclear strategic priorities; (5) the existing power configurations of managers who strive to preserve the existing balances and try to secure their interests, objectives, and positions.

The conditions for success reflected the barriers. Many employees stressed the necessity of openness on the objective and the method of the change. Great importance was attached to clear and regular information and there was a great need for truthful feedback of the information from the diagnosis. A significant proportion of the employees suggested that the ideas and opinions existing on all levels should be attentively listened to. Involvement of the employees in the changes and the contribution of practical experience of operating personnel were considered to be essential when searching for solutions to existing problems. The third success factor to be mentioned was that the process needed to be completed and that conclusions were to be drawn from the diagnosis, even if this would have consequences for the position of the top management and the line managers.

As a result of the barriers to change, specific attention was paid to the contribution by employees to the shaping of the social and technological aspect-system. Additionally, a process was started off to enhance management skills and to have the style of leadership fit in with the future form of organization. The communication on the change process was further strengthened and consultation between the top management and the work council was intensified.

Common Ground for Innovation

Employee task forces were set up to analyse the pressure points and to develop new ideas for the work organization. The task forces were guided and co-ordinated by an umbrella task group of employees and external advisers. Everyone could sign up for a task group with a theme related to his or her field of work. Additionally, people were directly invited to take part in these task groups. In total, some 200 employees in 25 task groups have tackled various pressure points and possibilities of improvement. Among other things, these task groups examined which improvements would yield an integration of the tasks. Team-oriented work on a completed production process was particularly considered. Placing the control of the information system and the applications under the unit operation was also considered because this would result in unity of time, place, and action. The task groups also studied how the customer-oriented service and the rendering of services could be enhanced, and how the development of the automated systems could be optimized. Specific task groups dealt with the culture and the desired style of leadership. Task groups with information analysts, information system designers, and employees of customer services and operations studied which demands were to be made by the user upon the new information system and what space was offered by the new information system for an optimal fit between the technological and social aspect-systems. The outcomes and the proposals from the task groups were compiled and translated by the umbrella task group into demands on the technological aspect-system and into proposals for redesigning business processes and the organizational structure. The desired culture has been made concrete in values and norms, and the desired style of leadership has been made operational in specific manners of behaviour and skills. All the proposals have been presented to the management, which, in consultation with the work council, took a final decision on the design of the new organization.

Some of the most important barriers to change were an unclear business strategy, inadequate management skills, and poor teamwork between managers of interdependent departments. A new set of cultural values was needed to encourage co-operation and teamwork. Also, reflection of the existing management style and renewal of leadership was necessary to realize an optimal fit between the organizational structure, the culture, and the style of leadership. To realize these objectives, a series of four conferences was organized for all the supervisors and managers. The number of participants to the conferences ranged from 30 to 60. The purpose of the conferences was to examine issues on strategy, organization, culture, and leadership from a variety of viewpoints, to learn from each other, and to develop common ground for change; in other words: What ideas and values do we share to bring about fundamental organizational change? During the conferences the participants analysed the data from the diagnosis from a variety of perspectives. As a result of the conferences, energy is directed towards resolving the issues at hand. New visions on strategy, culture, and business processes were developed. Introspection on leadership styles led to intense discussions about the hindrances put up by top management to real leadership and delegation of decision making. During the discussions on leadership styles, the criteria, qualifications, and preconditions for new leadership became clear.

The barriers to change indicated that communication was of vital importance to the realization of the change. During the change process, the entire organization was informed on the progress on a regular basis. Written communication took place via an information bulletin and the internal staff magazine. This information was sometimes general, but it was often also aimed at specific groups of employees, departments, or units. Besides written information, verbal communication was a recurrent part of the process. This provided an opportunity for the employees to ask questions. During the meetings, the top management played a clear role; by doing so, they not only indicated that they endorsed the necessity of the change but showed how important the contribution of the employees was to them. This manner of communicating demanded time and effort, but it proved to be an important means towards the progress of the process.

Innovation of Technology and Organization

The innovation of the technological aspect-system had already from the outset been primarily aimed at operating more swiftly to meet market demands and at increasing the efficiency. In the first instance, the technology is not regarded as a means to achieve organizational innovation. Different options regarding the technological as well as the organizational renewal were made debatable at an early stage. This working method had been stimulated by an early dialogue on the points of departure and designing philosophies for information technology and organization. Possible limitations within the technological aspect-system have put only minimal restrictions on the design of the social aspect-system. The information technology has been deployed as much as possible to support the organizational innovation. For instance, a division had been made within the system between the operating of the hardware and the operating of the applications. This division made it possible to assign the control of the payment traffic to the operations and to increase the control capacity of the teams. The new information system also offers possibilities for decentralized control and for the generation of management information. This allows for decision making at lower levels within the organization and a reduction in the number of management levels. Additionally, the new technology permits the teams to receive information on the results of their efforts. This also enables the teams to analyse the effectiveness of their activities and to improve their results while learning.

The innovation of the social aspect-system is based on teams dealing with a completed part of the business process. The teams carry out tasks that are logically linked. Executive tasks as well as steering and controlling tasks have been assigned to these teams. This way the teams have the possibility of taking action in the execution of their own work. In the operational functions, the teams deal with all the recurrent operations concerning the processing of specific information carriers, which had previously been separated. Moreover, the team carries out such tasks as the planning of the work, the monitoring of the schedule for payment processing and the primary maintenance of the equipment and the co-ordination of testing procedures, which permits a higher degree of autonomy than in the past. The on-line and real-time steering of payment processing enables the operation unit to steer and monitor the information and payment processing without interference from the computer department. The renewal of the information systems for payment processing and management information requires new ways of co-operation and project management in the development of information systems. The traditional division in information analyses, the formulation of functional requirements, the system development, the technical testing, and the implementation of new information systems is increasingly integrated and demands a new organizational form. The new department for computer services is composed of capacity teams with specific professional knowledge of information processing, network architecture, and hardware configurations. These teams are responsible for their own professional development and qualifications. The development of informational systems is fulfilled in multidisciplinary teams in which the various professionals and the users of the systems are working together under the supervision of a professional project manager. These teams are responsible for the realization of change in software configurations requested by other departments on a contractual basis with respect to results, cost, and planning. The professional teamwork reduces communication problems and makes demands on multidisciplinary co-operation by the specialists.

In the commercial functions, the information technology is used to improve the service to customers. All information processes to realize the commercial services have been integrated in an information system that supports the commercial functions. This renewal of information technology enables the integration of client-centred tasks. As a result, the clients have one office for all their requests and demands.

The most obvious result of the renewal of the information technology is the integration of tasks in teams and the arrangement of teams on the basis of market groups or processing related tasks. Less transfer of work and exchange of information contributes to a lesser degree of interdependence. Employees within the production and the professional and commercial teams can identify themselves more with the product or the service for which they are responsible. The new organization has three hierarchical levels: team manager, departmental manager, and management team.

For the implementation, conferences were conducted for each of the newly identified organizational departments and for all newly formed teams. During these conferences the tasks of the teams were clarified for all team members and the structure of the department was defined. Each team defined their goals, developed their team structure, identified a set of behaviours and values the team will abide by, and established a line for implementation. The new social aspect-system was implemented ahead of the new information system. This is to conform to the maxim: organize before you automatize. But the reasoning behind this was practical rather than ideological. The new information system was not ready to be implemented. Innovation of the social-aspect seemed to be easier and less expensive than renewal of information technology. At the time of writing this article, the information system has also been implemented.

DISCUSSION

The following conclusions, although roughly based on the case described above, are derived not only from the BGC case, but also on other studies of fundamental change (Boonstra, 1991; Boonstra, Steensma, Demenint, 1996). The conclusions focus on the relevance of the proposed sociotechnical framework, the barriers to change, and the relationship between fundamental change, design methodology, and participation.

Relevance of the Sociotechnical Framework

Sociotechnical system thinking provides a possibility for integration of institutional and transaction cost theories (organizations as open systems), theories about technological and organizational innovation (organizations as sociotechnical systems), and theories of planned change and organizational development (organizations as evolutionary and learning systems). The process of fundamental change in the BGC illustrated some of the integration among the three theoretical views within the sociotechnical framework.

Sociotechnical system theory looks upon organizations as open systems (Emery & Trist, 1965; Trist, 1981). The importance of environment and market demands for the performance and the continuity of the organization was illustrated. The need for businesses to develop a proactive business strategy and to realize flexible and innovative organizations was made clear. Cost reduction and customer satisfaction are no longer sufficient to be competitive. Developments in the environment, technological innovations, and market demands have become strong forces to abandon the classical paradigm of the maximal division of labour and to invest in teamwork that contributes to flexibility and innovation by learning principles of self-organization.

Sociotechnical system theory sees an interrelationship between the technological and social aspect-systems (Emery, 1969; Shani & Sena, 1994). In the BGC case it became clear that information technology can facilitate the transformation of organizations and that the technological aspect-system and the social aspect-system are strongly related. Renewal of information technology provided opportunities for fundamental changes in the social system. Organizational conservatism can be overcome when managers, information technologists, management consultants, and organizational members consciously make a choice for joint optimization of the technological and social systems. Information technology can facilitate the redesign of business processes and the transformation of structure, culture, leadership style, teams, and individuals. In this way it can contribute to the quality of working life.

Sociotechnical system theory emphasizes competence and self-learning capacities of organizations to realize continuous improvement. The theories of change are founded on group dynamics, learning processes, process intervention, and systematic change (Argyris, 1990; Beckhard, 1987; Beer & Walton, 1987; Schein, 1969). According to the sociotechnical change theories, the designing of organizations characterized by self-regulation and innovation can only take place when all members are involved in understanding and shaping their own work situation and are allowed to experience a learning process during the change process. The BGC case showed how concept creation, survey feedback, group discussions, self-designing task forces, and conferences were used to influence the design of the information technology and to realize a transformation of the social aspect-system from the perspective of a self-designing organization (Mohrman & Cummings, 1989).

It can be concluded that the sociotechnical system theory offers a solid framework for technological and organizational innovation. It also offers a strong theoretical alternative for business process redesign (BPR). Against the loose collection of non-theoretically founded ideas and techniques on corporate strategy, information technology, and organizational design of BPR, sociotechnical system theory puts forward a theory and methodology that is underpinned by psychological, sociological, and organizational theories and is anchored in a system theory that through the years has been further developed into concrete tools for fundamental organizational design and development. A further development of the sociotechnical system theory, however, is needed. Although the theory sees organizations as open systems, its concepts and methods for strategic development and implementation have been elaborated only slightly. First steps have been made by Emery (1987), Weisbord (1992), and Axelrod (1992), who suggest search conferences as a method for participative and interactive development of business policy and strategy. What is needed is a more elaborate theoretical foundation of strategic change and case studies on a deep level to analyse the methods and outcomes of strategic search conferences. Also, sociotechnical system theory has paid little attention to organizations as political systems when dealing with the actual transformation of organizations. In cases of fundamental change, several groups will try to influence the process of change towards an outcome that is favourable to them. Studies on power and influence in sociotechnical change projects have been made by Boonstra (1995) and Swan and Clark (1992), but further research into the relationship between the political aspect-system and the other aspect-systems in organizations is required. Case studies with a longitudinal dimension studying the politics of change processes for a period of time can add another layer to the theory of sociotechnical change.

Barriers to Change

Innovation of information technology and organizational structures is a complex process of fundamental change. The BGC case shows us that these innovation processes meet several hindrances that must be overcome.

It is important to realize that none of the organizational members in the BGC case attribute impediments to change to the information technology. It seemed that information technology could even promote a fundamental transformation of the entire organizational system. The impediments to change were not related to information technology but to the social aspect-system.

The existing division of labour and poor interfunctional teamwork is an important barrier to change. The BGC case made clear that the division of labour inhibits the division's and teams' ability to learn, because they do not possess all the information necessary to solve problems. The division of labour makes it difficult to see and analyse the entire problem. As a result, solutions are made on an *ad hoc* basis and are directed at the realization of sub-tasks of a single department. The detailed division of tasks often results in competition, misunderstandings, and conflicts between departments because people in different departments have a limited understanding of what goes on in the organization. Different patterns of behaviour and expectations develop while the specialized and confined operations do not encourage co-operation and interfunctional teamwork.

Behaviour in organizations is closely related to norms and values. The norms and values originate from the socialization process, education, and conventions of the organization. The BGC case shows that norms and values limit people's choice of behavioural alternatives and, hence, people's ability to change. Managers in particular have difficulties with changes in norms and values, because they have come to think of their position and behaviour as suitable. What appears from the BGC case is that cultural aspects and management behaviour are closely related and can yield serious impediments to change. Work conference can support a shift in cultural values and norms and stimulate new styles of leadership.

Resistance to organizational and cultural changes can primarily be expected within the management. The BGC case made clear that managers could be cultural defenders because the existing culture serves as an instrument to give meaning to incidents and events in a way consistent with their conception of the work organization, the work situation, and the people employed. Understanding of environmental changes helped to broaden the perspective. Based on the acquired understanding of the market and the product, the business strategy could be discussed and specified so that a shared value-system could emanate from the organization. The top management's role was to disseminate new norms and values concerning the manners of behaviour, desired and undesired actions, communication, important activities and events, the way operations should be conducted, and the style of management.

Forces in the organization to preserve the existing balance of power can hinder the change process. In the process, different coalitions will direct their attention to securing their interests, objectives, and power positions (Kanter, 1993). It is, therefore, imperative to consider the power processes during change processes (Pfeffer, 1992). At the start of the change process in the BGC case, the top management neglected to translate general objectives into concrete measures. Line management, being uncertain about their new position within the organization, were enabled to pursue their own objectives and hindered concrete changes. In the middle levels of the organization, groups or coalitions were developing which did not contribute to fundamental changes in culture and organization. With respect to the power and political processes, an important prerequisite for a successful change process is that the largest support possible should be generated in the earliest stage possible. Interviews, questionnaires, and work conferences were methods to realize a large support for innovation.

The way decision making is organized contributes to the success of change with respect to organizational innovation. The respondents in the case research attached much value to the participation of the members of the organization in the problem analysis, the designation of the objectives of change, and the choices for innovation. Making a clear and well-informed decision on innovation and the communication thereof is essential. The BGC case shows that facilitating problem analyses and application of ideas of operating personnel and an open consultation about solutions and alternative supports the change process. It is apparent that an in-depth problem analysis will take much time and effort. The question arises whether this investment is really necessary when there is a clear idea of the problems and the possible solutions among the members of a design team. The case shows that participation of all members of the organization in the decision-making process can contribute positively to the change process. By gaining experience with problem solving, change processes, and organizational development, organization members gradually learn to shape changes and react flexibly to changing circumstances on their own.

There is no standard approach for the innovation of information technology and organizational development. Each and every change process has its own characteristics. Therefore, a reflection of the change objectives and the way the change process can be approached is required: managing the process for change. Because change processes often develop unpredictably, it is required to monitor the course of events and to intervene when necessary. In the BGC case the management of change was the responsibility of a co-ordinating team consisting of employees and external consultants, which facilitated the change process. It seemed that proper information flow during the process is essential for a good development of the changes. Resistance to change does not solely stem from the attempt to keep the situation stable and secure, but originates principally from the lack of clarity about the change objectives and the approach to change process (Beer, Eisenstat, & Spector, 1990). Communication with the members of the organization during the change process is of essential importance for the reduction of uncertainty, and the visualization of advancements in the process. It is meaningful to plan the approach to the change process thoroughly in advance, and make an inventory of the possibilities and impediments to the change process. This concerns the existing views on change, interests, power relations, the support for change, and impediments within the organization's structure, culture, and style of management.

The Dilemma of Designing and Developing

Competence and self-learning seem to be critical elements of technological and organizational innovation. A development approach can initiate these learning processes, but, in order to be successful, common values, willingness to co-operate, a clear vision on the business processes, and clarity as to the reasons for changes are needed. The BGC case indicates that organizations with a strong division of labour and predominantly bureaucratic characteristics cannot meet these conditions for learning and development. The BGC organization was unable to follow development and learning processes independently because the learning approach is contrary to the methods that had been used for years to analyse and solve problems.

A dilemma is created by fundamentally changing organizations. The expert-design approach offers possibilities for radically redesigning the organization and drastic and revolutionary change. Business process re-design claims to achieve dramatic performance improvements by using a design approach with linear steering from the top, tasks forces of management, and the contribution of business consultants. At the same time, many projects aimed at redesign of organizations do not yield the desired outcomes. It is estimated that three-quarters of the re-engineering projects fail (Davenport, 1993). With the design approach it becomes difficult to contribute to the realization of self-managing teams and the enhancement of the organizational learning ability. The development approach is preferred in the case of fundamental changes, but is often appears to be difficult to break with traditionally-shaped organizations when only the development strategy is used. The BGC case give some ideas on how to deal with this dilemma between designing and developing organizations. The basic assumptions for innovation and change were formulated in work conferences and discussed between top management and work council. After sanctioning the basic assumptions by top management, the analysis of the organization can be executed by a facilitating team with the co-operation of all members involved. However, the knowledge of an expert is often necessary to ensure an integral diagnosis and to prohibit signalled problems from being immediately solved according to the existing principles, patterns, and procedures. The interpretation of data can take place in a participative learning process, but a contribution of a change agent is necessary to establish procedures, guide meetings, and discussions, and to clarify the relationships in the data. After the diagnosis, it often appears to be difficult to develop a new work organization in co-operation with all the organization members, because there is often a divided culture, distrust, different objectives, and conflicts of interest. The subdivision of labour has alienated the organization's members from their product, the market, and the mission of the organization, and they do not see the entire transformation process. New organizational forms are difficult to envision, and the willingness jointly to develop this understanding is often insufficiently present. Apparently, the prerequisites for employing a development approach in which the organization is shaped from the bottom up in a participative way are not met. The dilemma could be solved by alternating between the formulation of co-ordinating and innovative frameworks and the interpretation of these frameworks from the bottom up. As the process progresses, the emphasis gradually shifts to the development approach in which the organization's members manage the changes themselves.

CONCLUSION

Technological and organizational innovation needs a theoretical framework to understand the relationships between strategy, technology, and organization and to overcome organizational conservatism and guide the change process. The contemporary sociotechnical system theory offers such a framework. The theory provides a base of knowledge for redesigning organizations as well as developing organizations by learning processes. In this respect the theory is more funded, mature, and helpful than the loose collection of insights and methods of business process redesign. However, further development of the sociotechnical system theory is needed, specifically in the field of strategic development and issues concerned with barriers, power, and influence during fundamental change.

Information technologies offer opportunities for organizational innovation and could contribute to the flexibility and innovative capacity of organizations. It also creates the potential for increasing the quality of working life. Impediments to technological and organizational innovation are seldom related to the technological system. Barriers to innovation and reasons for organizational conservatism are to be found in the social system. Case research indicates six barriers in the social system itself: the existing division of labour and poor interfunctional teamwork; the norms and values limiting people's ability to change; top-down leadership and poor vertical communication; inadequate management skills; the existing power configuration; and lastly a linear and formal process of decision making on innovation. Successful innovation needs a process of learning to analyse market demands and organizational problems and to design information systems, business processes, and work organization by self-designing teams and dedicated management of the change process.

Competence and self-learning appear to be crucial elements of technological and organizational innovation. The participative development approach initiates and stimulates these learning processes, but at the same time interferes with the change process because people find it difficult to be objective towards the existing situation and to form an idea of a completely new situation. An expert design approach seems to offer possibilities for

radical and revolutionary change. Nevertheless, many design projects fail because fundamental change is not a programme, but a learning process. The dilemma between designing and developing organizations can possibly be solved by alternating between a top-down formulation of goals and co-ordination of the change process and bottom-up self-designing activities in which organizational members manage the change process themselves.

ACKNOWLEDGEMENTS

The authors would like to thank Rob Leliveld for his support in case research, Interpay-BGC for access to case studies, and SANT for research funds.

REFERENCES

Ansoff, H.I. (1985). *Implanting strategic management*. Englewood Cliffs, NJ: Prentice Hall.

Argyris, C. (1983). Action science and intervention. *Journal of Applied Behavioral Science, 43*(5), 115–140.

Argyris, C. (1990). *Overcoming organizational defenses: Facilitating organizational learning*. Boston, Mass.: Allyn & Bacon.

Ashby, W.R. (1969). Self-regulation and requisite variety. In F.E. Emery (Ed.), *Systems thinking*. London: Penguin Books.

Axelrod, D. (1992). Getting everyone involved: How one organization involved its employees, supervisors, and managers in redesigning the organization. *Journal of Applied Behavioral Science, 28*(4), 499–509.

Beckhard, R. (1987). Strategies for large systems change. In W.A. Pasmore & J.J. Sherwood (Eds.), *Sociotechnical systems: A sourcebook*. San Diego, Calif.: University Associates.

Beer, M. (1988). The critical path for change: Keys to success and failure in six companies. In R.H. Killmann & T.J. Covin (Eds.), *Revitalizing organizations for a competitive world*. San Francisco, Calif.: Jossey-Bass.

Beer, M., Eisenstat, R.A., & Spector, B. (1990). *The critical path to corporate renewal*. Boston, Mass.: Harvard.

Beer, M., & Walton, A.E. (1987). Organization change and development. *Annual Review of Psychology, 38*, 339–367.

Beinum, H.J.J. van. (1990). *Participative democracy*. Leiden, Germany: University Press.

Boonstra, J.J. (1991). *Integrale organisatie-ontwikkeling: Vormgeven aan fundamentele veranderingsprocessen* [Integral organizational development: Managing fundamental change processes in organizations]. Utrecht, The Netherlands: Lemma.

Boonstra, J.J. (1995). The use of power and influence tactics in change processes. In J.J. Boonstra (Ed.), *Power dynamics and organizational changes*. Leuven, Belgium: EAWOP.

Boonstra, J.J., Steensma, H.O., & Demenint, M.I. (1996). *Ontwerden en ontwikkelen van organisaties [Designing and developing organizations]*. Utrecht, The Netherlands: Lemma.

Cherns, A. (1987). The principles of sociotechnical design revisited. *Human Relations, 29*(8), 783–792.

Child, J., & Loveridge, R. (1990). *Information technology in European service: Towards a micro-electronic future*. Oxford: Basil Blackwell.

Clark, P.A., & Staunton, N. (1989). *Innovations in technology and organization*. London: Routledge.

Davenport, T.H. (1993). *Process innovation: Reengineering work through information technology*. Boston, Mass.: Harvard.

Emery, F.E. (1959). *Characteristics of sociotechnical systems*. London: Tavistock.

Emery, F.E. (1969). *Systems thinking*. London: Penguin Books.

Emery, F.E., & Trist, E.L. (1965). The causal texture of organizational environment. *Human Relations, 20*(1), 21–32.

Emery, M. (1987). *The theory and practice of search conferences*. Paper presented at the Einar Thorsrud Memorial Symposium, Oslo.

Freeman, R.E. (1984). *Strategic management: A stakeholder approach*. Boston, Mass.: Pittman.

Guha, S., Kettinger, W.J., & Teng, J.T.C. (1993). Business process redesign: Building a comprehensive methodology. *Information Systems Management, Summer*, 13–22.

Hammer, M., & Champy, J. (1993). *Reengineering the corporation: A manifesto for business revolution*. New York: Harper.

Harrison, B.D., & Pratt, M.D. (1993). Reengineering business processes. *Planning Review, 9*(2), 53–61.

Herbst, P.G. (1976). *Alternatives to hierarchies*. Leiden, Germany: Martinus Nijhoff.

Kanter, R.M. (1993). *The change masters: Corporate entrepreneurs at work* (2nd ed.). London: Routledge.

Mohrman, S.A., & Cummings, T.G. (1989). *Self-designing organizations: Learning how to create high performance*. Reading, Mass.: Addison-Wesley.

Pasmore, W.A. (1988). *Designing effective organizations: Sociotechnical system perspective*. New York: Wiley.

Pava, C.H. (1986). Redesigning sociotechnical system design: Concepts and methods for the 1990s. *Journal of Applied Behavioral Science, 22*(3), 201–221.

Pfeffer, J. (1992). *Managing with power: Politics and influence in organizations*. Boston, Mass.: Harvard.

Schein, E.H. (1969). *Process consultation: Its role in organization development*. Reading, Mass.: Addison-Wesley.

Shani, A.B.R., & Sena, J.A. (1994). Information technology and the integration of change: Sociotechnical system approach. *Journal of Applied Behavioral Science, 30*(2), 247–270.

Susman, G.I. (1976). *Autonomy at work: A sociotechnical analysis of participative management*. New York: Praeger.

Swan, J.A., & Clark, P. (1992). Organizational decision making in the appropriation of technological innovation: Cognitive and political dimensions. *The European Work and Organizational Psychologist, 2*(2), 103–127.

Trist, E.L. (1981). *The evolution of sociotechnical systems: A conceptual framework and an action research program*. Ontario, Canada: The Quality of Working Life Center.

Trist, E.L. (1982). Sociotechnical system perspective. In A.H. van der Ven & W.F. Joyce (Eds.), *Perspectives on organization design and behavior*. New York: Wiley.

Turner, A.N., & Lawrence, P.R. (1965). *Industrial jobs and the worker: An investigation of response to task attributes*. Boston, Mass.: Harvard.

Walton, R.E. (1988). *Up and running: Integrating information technology and the organizations*. Boston, Mass.: Harvard.

Weick, K. (1990). Technology as an equivoque: Sense making in new technologies. In P.S. Goodman & L.S. Sproull (Eds.), *Technology and organizations*. San Francisco, Calif.: Jossey-Bass.

Weisbord, M.R. (1992). *Discovering common ground*. San Francisco, Calif.: Berrett-Koehler.

EUROPEAN JOURNAL OF WORK AND ORGANIZATIONAL PSYCHOLOGY, 1996, 5 (3), 377–397

Stress and Technological Innovation:
A Comparative Study of Design Practices and
Implementation Strategies

David G. Wastell

*Department of Computer Science, University of Manchester,
Manchester, UK*

Cary L. Cooper

*Manchester School of Management, University of Manchester Institute of
Science and Technology, Manchester, UK*

The implementation of new technology in the workplace is a highly problematic process. New computer systems are often associated with adverse
changes in the quality of working life: raised stress levels, impaired job satisfaction, increased routinization, and so on. This article reports a comparative
analysis of two projects involving the computerization of control-room operations in two ambulance services: London and Manchester. The two outcomes
were strikingly different. In the London case, severe operational problems
led to the abandonment of the project. In contrast, the article reports a psychophysiological evaluation of the Manchester project which showed that the new
system led to both superior service levels and to reduced levels of stress. In
particular, it was shown that control staff responded to high levels of workload
with lower systolic blood pressure and subjective anxiety.

The contrasting outcomes of the two projects are attributed to two main
sets of factors: managerial and technical. The technical design philosophy at
Manchester was "user centred"; it embraced what may be called a "tool
paradigm", where the aim of technological innovation is to support and
augment the role of the human operator. In contrast, the London project was
highly Tayloristic, with the accent on replacing unreliable human labour by
an automated system. The way the implementation process was managed at
Manchester (strong leadership, user involvement) was also notably different
from the London experience (weak project management, poor industrial relations). These findings suggest that human-centred principles can provide a
highly effective foundation for design, but careful management of the implementation process is also required if IT projects are to be brought to successful
fruition.

Requests for reprints should be addressed to Dr D.G. Wastell, Department of Computer
Science, University of Manchester, Oxford Road, Manchester M13 9PL, UK.

INTRODUCTION

The implementation of IT systems in the workplace is a troublesome process in which the record of success is ingloriously low. All too many IT projects fail. Lyytinen (1988) reports a failure rate of at least 50% and other pundits have put the figure much higher (Gladden, 1982; Laudon & Laudon, 1991). There are many ways in which projects miscarry. They may run over budget or beyond time-scales. Many systems are abandoned before implementation and, of those that are implemented, rejection may occur because they fail to deliver expected operational/business benefits, or for other reasons they are technically unsatisfactory or organizationally inappropriate.

The prevalence of failure in IT projects has spurred much research into those critical factors that dispose projects to a successful outcome (e.g. Lucas, 1981). By an IT project, we mean an innovation process involving several phases (Sauer, 1993) through which a technical product is first developed, then implemented in the workplace, and finally incorporated into routine operation. Crudely we may divide success factors into two main groups: product factors and process factors. The former category refers to the technical quality of the artifact, namely the degree to which the computer-based system satisfies the user's technical needs, the usability of the software, and so forth. The technical merit of a system on its own is, however, not enough to guarantee successful implementation. IT projects are highly political events. New systems typically entail considerable organizational upheaval; old work practices and job roles are often the subject of radical redefinition (Wastell & Newman, 1993). Unless these change processes are carefully managed, projects may easily run aground. Failure to involve end-users in the development process, for instance, may engender alienation, resistance, and ultimately rejection (Lucas, 1981). Two process factors have consistently been shown to have a strong bearing on project outcome: top management support and user involvement (Laudon & Laudon, 1991; Wastell & Sewards, 1995).

One of the most public failures of a computerized system in the UK occurred in late 1992. On 27th October, the national television channels announced the breakdown of a computerized command-and-control system operated by the London Ambulance Service (LAS). As a result of this failure, it was feared that many lives had been lost due to the late or non-arrival of emergency ambulances. As a result of pressure in Parliament and a vociferous press campaign, a public enquiry was put in place by the Government in order to determine the reasons for the breakdown. The resulting report (Page, Williams, & Boyd, 1993) is a damning but impressively thorough post-mortem of the LAS disaster.

Both product and process deficiencies were prominent in the LAS fiasco. Superficially, the project failed because software had been incompletely tested and was incapable of handling the volume of traffic experienced at peak levels: system response times became unacceptably long, status errors accumulated, and job queues eventually grew out of control, ultimately producing the breakdown. At a more fundamental level were a range of serious management failures. Requirements for the system had been inadequately specified, user training was weak and poorly timed, and project management was conspicuous by its absence. Most telling of all, the hostile industrial relations climate in LAS had exerted a pervasive corrosive influence on the project. Mistrust of the workforce, together with outside pressures to complete the work quickly, had led management to run the project in a highly autocratic mode. Little involvement of the workforce had occurred; legitimate concerns expressed by staff were dismissed as politically motivated subversion (Page et al., 1993). Despite warning signs, management had pressed on with a system that appeared to be technically suspect, with a final result that had all the inevitability of a Greek tragedy. Undoubtedly, classic "counter-implementation tactics" (Hirschheim, 1985, p. 164) on the part of an alienated workforce had also contributed to the failure; ambulance staff were, for instance, suspected of pressing the wrong buttons on their cabin consoles, thus feeding erroneous status information into the central database.

There are many examples of failed projects in the research literature (Lyytinen, 1988); successful initiatives are less often described. Thus far we have examined a particularly spectacular example of failure. In the rest of the article we will describe a technically similar project in another ambulance service, the Greater Manchester Ambulance Service (GMAS). This project has been the subject of an intensive longitudinal field study carried out by the authors. As will be seen, the GMAS project, far from failing, was a noteworthy success.

The goals of the research in GMAS were twofold: to monitor the conduct of the development process and to perform a comprehensive psycho-physiological evaluation of the impact of the computerized system. A salient feature of the evaluation was the equal weight that it gave to changes in the health and well-being of users, as well as changes in their productivity and efficiency. This emphasis is important. The research literature has tended to associate computerization with adverse changes in working conditions (Gale & Christie, 1987; Zuboff, 1982), in particular, with increased stress (Bramwell & Cooper, 1995; Briner & Hockey, 1988; Kahn & Cooper, 1986; Nelson & Kletke, 1990; Patrickson, 1986). There is, of course, no causal necessity in this (Frese, 1987b; Zapf, 1993). The question is one of design, both of the technology itself and of the embedding work organization (Blackler & Brown, 1986; Turner & Karasek, 1984). Indeed the potential of technology to improve the quality of work-life forms the basis of certain design philosophies (see, for instance: Frese, 1987a; Hacker, 1987;

Mumford, 1986). In reality, though, design practices do not embody such ideals; they are typically Tayloristic, emphasizing efficiency over user well-being (Blackler & Brown, 1986; Clegg, Waterson, & Carey, 1994).

The impact of computerization on the psychological welfare of operators was thus an important concern in the GMAS study, and led to our adoption of a psychophysiological methodology in order to measure stress levels object-ively under real operational conditions. The essence of the psychophysio-logical approach lies in the meshing of complementary perspectives (Gale & Christie, 1987): i.e. that a complete account of psychological phenomena requires the triangulation of three key dimensions: (1) behaviour (e.g. job performance in relation to external demands), (2) physiology (e.g. auto-nomic nervous system responses indicative of stress), and (3) subjective experience (feelings of anxiety and strain). The use of psychophysiology in research on IT has been advocated by a number of writers (Gale & Christie, 1987; Wastell, 1990). Although there is a relatively long tradition of labor-atory psychophysiology in this area, field studies are much rarer. Examples of laboratory investigations include Kuhman's (1989) study of the stressful effects of slow system-response times, and Sundelin and Hagberg's (1989) study of pause times in VDU work. Two examples of field investigations are Johansson and Aronsson's (1984) widely quoted study of computer-mediated office work and Brown, Wastell, and Copeman's (1982) study of technological/organizational change in British Telecom.

Of the wide range of psychophysiological parameters (EEG-based indices, electrodermal measures, adrenal hormones, etc.) that were con-sidered as candidates for the study, the decision was made to focus on cardiovascular measures. One reason was practical, namely that a feasible means was available to record heart rate and blood pressure with minimal intrusion under operational conditions. The key role played by the cardio-vascular system in the body's response to stressful situations provided a more fundamental reason for the choice. When faced with an external challenge or threat, organisms may respond in one of two ways: passively (denial/avoidance of the challenge) or actively (real engagement with the situation). "Active coping" involves a general mobilization of the body's resources, orchestrated by the sympathetic nervous system, in which cardio-vascular activation plays a central role. This is manifested by increases in both heart rate and systolic blood pressure, the latter reflecting an increase in the "pumping force" of the heart (Turner, 1994). The sensitivity of both these parameters to short-term changes in task demands has been well estab-lished in experimental tasks (Obrist, 1981; Turner, 1994); this makes them especially suitable for a real-time role. Blood pressure is also of relevance from a health perspective as there is suggestive evidence of a link between excessive short-term reactivity in blood pressure and long-term propensity to stress-related illness, such as hypertensive heart disease (Turner, 1994).

To recapitulate, we will report in this article a psychophysiological field study of the implementation of an ambulance command-and-control system. Ambulance command-and-control work is highly demanding. Lives depend upon the efficient and expeditious decisions of human operators. In this environment, stress is a crucial issue and any changes that exacerbate the already stressful nature of the job would be disastrous; on the other hand, if computer support were effective in reducing stress, this would be of immense value. The GMAS project will be described in the next section, followed by a detailed account of the results of the psychophysiological evaluation. A discussion of the key reasons for the success of the project, using the LAS case as a comparison, will complete the article.

THE MANCHESTER AMBULANCE STUDY

Context

Greater Manchester is a densely populated, largely urban area covering around 500 square miles with a population of approximately 2.7 million. The emergency ambulance service for this area is provided by the Greater Manchester Ambulance Service (GMAS) who operate a fleet of around 65 highly equipped ambulances (often with paramedical support). These ambulances are based at a number of ambulance stations dispersed across the Manchester area. The movements of the ambulances are co-ordinated by a control centre in downtown Manchester. The computer project involved the implementation of a computerized command-and-control system (called ALERT) in this control room.

The "Command-and-Control" Process

The fundamental nature of the command-and-control process is as follows. In essence, the process involves two distinct stages: call reception and ambulance despatching. These stages are handled by two main staff groups in the control centre: the call-takers and the despatchers, with the latter being responsible for controlling the movement of ambulances. We will first describe the process as it operated prior to computerization before commenting on the way that ALERT has changed the situation.

The command-and-control process begins with receipt of a "999" telephone call. Before computerization, call-takers took down details of each call (location and type of incident, etc.) on a paper form, the "Call Receipt Record" (CRR), and the CRR was then handed to the appropriate despatcher (according to geographical location). Having decided which ambulance is best placed to deal with the case, the process then requires the despatcher to contact the appropriate ambulance station and an ambulance is mobilized. Having reached the scene of the incident, the crew carry out any immediate action that is required and the patient is conveyed to a hospital "Accident and Emergency" department. When an incident is complete, the despatcher typically instructs the ambulance to return to base.

Communication between despatchers and ambulances was (and still is) mediated via a combination of the telephone and a radio link. An important feature is the use of a small panel of buttons in the ambulance cabin to transmit standard signals back to the control centre in order to provide information on the ambulance's changing status. These buttons cause messages to appear on a small display unit indicating the time at which the ambulance leaves its base, the time of arrival at the incident, etc. These pieces of information are vital and, prior to computerization, the despatcher was required to transcribe the information manually from the screen onto a "plotting chart" (an A3 chart used to record the movements and disposition of ambulances) and also onto the CRR.

The introduction of ALERT has not fundamentally changed the general structure of the command-and-control process. The main change is that communication between call-takers and despatchers is now mediated by a database. Instead of filling out the CRR, call-takers now type the requisite information directly into the ALERT database. Jobs are then routed by the system to the appropriate despatcher. For their part, despatchers sit in front of a VDU screen on which a "job queue" is displayed; this is simply a list of outstanding jobs ordered by time from which they select the job that they wish to handle next. Another significant change is that the status messages from the ambulances are now automatically captured and recorded in the database. This constitutes a major benefit, especially when despatchers are busy, as this activity used to take up a significant degree of attention.

Besides the integrated radio link, ALERT was expected to yield a number of further significant benefits. ALERT assists, for example, in establishing the definitive location of incidents by providing both an on-line street-finder and a thesaurus of well-known landmarks (e.g. public houses). This ensures that only validated locations are entered onto the database, which can help save much wasted time at the despatching stage. For each location, the database also contains a record of the nearest three ambulance stations; these "nearest response sets" are intended to help despatchers to select which ambulance to use. ALERT also provides a number of other supportive information displays, e.g. an electronic version of the plotting chart.

A Brief History of the Computer Project

The computer project was formally inaugurated in late 1992 and, after an unsatisfactory opening period, it got properly underway in mid-1993. A project manager (PC) from within the service with the requisite combination of technical and managerial skills was appointed to run the project as his full-time responsibility. From the outset, PC took a firm hold on the technical side of the work, engaging in extensive and thorough negotiations with the software providers (a small software house) in order to ensure that the system exactly satisfied GMAS's requirements and was consonant with their working practices.

On the user side, the importance of keeping control room staff well-informed and up to date with progress was recognized by PC. Various methods were used for this purpose: e.g. a newsletter entitled *ALERT Update*. It was also attempted, within limits, to involve staff in the development of the system, e.g. they defined the "nearest response sets" and were given scope to include information in the system which would be of help to them, e.g. the position of emergency telephones on the motorway network.

Live implementation of ALERT was scheduled for the early summer of 1994. The implementation period was recognized as a critical time requiring thorough and adroit management. A comprehensive training programme was executed in the early part of 1994. The control staff were provided with well-designed, individually customized user manuals. The successful execution of a series of live trials was also used to build up confidence in the system and to test it under real operational conditions.

Considerable tension and anxiety were revealed during the live trials. The manager of the control centre commented:

> There was a great deal of apprehension at first . . . people didn't trust the system . . . they would put a call in and walk down the room to check that it was in. We didn't remove all the visual aids like the plotting sheet . . . it's their comfort blanket. A lot of people didn't want the system, they feared it would make their job harder. Now they all want it . . . they didn't want it switched off at the end of the trial.

The thoroughness of the training, the care taken in tailoring the design of the system, and the carefully staggered implementation period helped to ensure that the "switch over" to computerized operation, carried out in June 1994, was a success. No significant major problems were encountered and the system has been in continuous routine operation since this date.

Subjects and Research Design

The primary goal of the research was to perform a psychophysiological evaluation of the impact of ALERT by comparing job performance and stress before and after implementation. The study thus involved two phases of data collection, the pre-implementation baseline and the post-implementation review. The baseline phase was performed in January/February 1994. This was as close to implementation as was possible without encroaching on the training period. Post-implementation data was collected in October/November 1994. This was roughly four months after implementation. At this time, ALERT had been running smoothly for several months and was well bedded in.

Each of the two data collection phases lasted around six weeks. Due to university commitments, visits to the control centre were constrained to the morning period, between 9.00AM and 1.00PM, with data being collected at hourly intervals. This was an opportune time as extremes of workload characteristically appeared during this period, with demands picking up from a low level at the beginning of the morning to a peak around lunchtime.

The control room was manned by five shifts of operators, each shift typically comprising four despatchers and four call-takers, working under the direction of two supervisors and a duty manager. Each shift was visited on two separate days in different working weeks. Typically, these days were in consecutive weeks, although the interval was sometimes longer as a result of the vagaries of the shift system. In total, around 50 operational staff worked in the control room (numbers inevitably fluctuated over the course of the study): 90% were female; age range was 19–55, with a mean of 24 years (i.e. predominantly young women).

Dependent and Independent Variables

The evaluation framework involved a combination of "off-line" questionnaire measures and real-time monitoring of performance and physiology. In order to assess general levels of job satisfaction and occupational stress, Cooper, Sloan, and Williams' (1988) Occupational Stress Indicator (OSI) was administered during the baseline phase for completion at home. The OSI is an extensive questionnaire (see Table 1) enabling the assessment of a broad range of job-related sources of pressure (independent variables) and their putative effects on well-being (job satisfaction, mental/physical health). Relevant "moderating" attributes (e.g. type A behaviour, control) are also assessed. A considerable body of normative data is available which provides a useful reference for comparison. The OSI's construct validity and reliability have been established (Robertson, Cooper, & Williams, 1990) and the instrument also appears to have significant predictive validity (Rees & Cooper, 1991).

It should be emphasized that the OSI was administered only once during the study, in the baseline phase. The OSI is a large document which provides a broad-ranging, general profile of an organization from a stress perspective. Many of the issues addressed by the OSI were outside the design scope of the computer system (e.g. personnel policies), and cause–effect relationships would have been difficult to infer given the level of generality of the OSI. The OSI was thus administered just once in order to provide a baseline profile. For the follow-up phase a simple questionnaire was developed

TABLE 1
Occupational Stress Indicator

Primary Scale	Subscale	GMAS	Population Norms
Job satisfaction	Achievement and growth	17.8 (4.0)	21.3 (5.8)
	The job itself: tasks and functions	14.5 (2.6)	16.4 (3.2)
	Management style	15.3 (2.6)	16.4 (4.3)
	Motivation and autonomy	14.0 (2.5)	15.3 (3.8)
	Personal relationships	10.9 (2.0)	11.6 (2.5)
State of health	Mental	56.1 (12.0)	55.5 (13.0)
	Physical	37.1 (8.2)	29.8 (9.7)
Personality	Type A behaviour: competitive and thrusting	16.6 (3.3)	17.7 (3.9)
	Need for achievement	10.7 (2.0)	11.2 (2.3)
Locus of control	Low influence over events	19.3 (2.4)	18.6 (2.9)
	Low influence over others	11.4 (1.9)	10.5 (2.2)
Sources of stress	Unsatisfactory job demands: hours and variety of work	31.6 (5.3)	30.2 (6.5)
	Problematic relationships with others	31.4 (7.3)	30.3 (7.5)
	Unsatisfactory career prospects and rewards	30.0 (6.9)	28.4 (8.1)
	An unsupportive organizational environment	45.0 (7.1)	38.9 (9.2)
	Conflict between home and work	25.3 (6.9)	30.1 (10.0)

Mean values are shown for both GMAS control room staff and population norms; standard deviations are given in parentheses.

focusing on: (1) the impact of ALERT on issues such as motivation, stress, and health; (2) its technical quality; and (3) management's handling of the implementation process (see Table 2).

As well as the questionnaires, a set of real-time measures was collected in order to determine the relationship between work demands and psychological strain during live operational conditions. This assessment focused exclusively on the despatching task. Despatchers are very much at the "sharp end" of the command-and-control process and the effects of ALERT on their work thus constituted the most decisive test of its effectiveness. The work of the despatchers is also more homogenous than that of the other categories of staff: they perform a well-defined and highly focused task, whereas call-takers, for instance, tend to perform other duties (e.g. clerical tasks) as well as receiving calls. Satisfactory data was obtained for 18 despatchers (i.e. a set of observations reflecting a representative range of workloads).

Specifically, the following information was collected. External work demands were measured by counting the number of simultaneously active

TABLE 2
The Post-implementation Questionnaire

General Area	Specific Issue	Significance (χ^2 test)
Section I: Impact of ALERT	Job satisfaction	12.2, $P < 0.001$
	Skill variety	9.8, $P < 0.01$
	Job motivation	NS
	Career aspirations	NS
	State of mental health	NS
	State of physical health	NS
	Pressure during a typical day	NS
	Ability to cope with work	NS
	Tiredness at end of shift	NS
	Situational awareness	NS
Section II: Implementation Process	Quality of training	2.8, $P < 0.10$
	User involvement in design	NS
	Management's handling of implementation	NS
Section III: Technical quality of ALERT	Usability	6.0, $P < 0.05$
	Reliability and "trustworthiness"	NS
	Effectiveness (helps do the job better)	10.6, $P < 0.01$
	Improvement compared to paper system	14.7, $P < 0.001$

Operators were asked a range of *post hoc* questions regarding: the impact of the computer system on their work (Section I); their satisfaction with the implementation process (Section II); the technical quality of the system (Section III). All sections used a five-point scale. For Section I, the scale ran from "a big improvement" (+2) at one extreme, through "no change" (0), to "much worse" (−2). For Sections II and III, the scale ranged from "very satisfied" (+2) to "very dissatisfied" (−2). Statistical analyses were carried out using one sample chi-square tests.

"jobs" being handled by the despatcher at the time of sampling, i.e. a quantitative measure of workload. The psychophysiological response to these external pressures was measured using a combination of cardio-vascular and subjective measures. Two cardiovascular parameters were measured (heart rate and blood pressure) using an OMRON HEM-815F digital BP monitor. This device is simply slipped onto the left index finger and enables cardiovascular state to be determined with minimal intrusion (operators were able to continue with their work, using their right-hand only). The monitor uses the oscillometric technique to determine blood pressure, the validity of which has been established by Light, Obrist, and Cubeddu (1988). At the same time, two aspects of subjective state were assessed: anxiety and fatigue. These two dimensions were measured by asking staff to make a mark on each of two visual analogue scales indicating how anxious and tired they felt. The two poles of the anxiety scale were "relaxed" and "anxious"; for fatigue, "alert" and "tired". This simple technique has been found practical and effective in other real-time studies (Brown et al., 1982; Wastell, Brown, & Copeman, 1982). The analogue scores were converted to a numerical scale from 0 to 10.

RESULTS

The Occupational Stress Indicator

Table 1 presents the main results of the OSI analysis. Of the 40 question-naires distributed, 22 were returned. In general, there are few differences between the GMAS averages and the population benchmarks; however, some salient deviations are present. Regarding job satisfaction, the OSI provides evidence of significant dissatisfaction with the potential of control room work for personal growth and development. Although mental health was apparently in line with that of the population at large, there was evidence that the physical health of control room staff (sleeplessness, headaches, tiredness, etc.) was significantly worse than the general average. Control room work involves an arduous mixture of day and night shift work which undoubtedly accounts for much of the apparent level of physical ill-health (Warr, 1987).

There was no evidence that control room staff differ from the general population in terms of "locus of control", nor that they differ in terms of their type A behavioural tendencies (i.e. the hard-driving, ambitious personality syndrome that is associated with higher stress levels; Wastell & Newman, 1993). Sources of stress were also broadly in line with the general norm, although there was evidence that staff found the "organizational environment" generally unsupportive, i.e. that staffing levels, training, and senior management back-up were, in general, felt to be inadequate.

The Impact of ALERT on Service Performance

Standards for the performance of ambulance services are laid down centrally by the National Health Service. The key performance indicator is the time taken from call receipt to an ambulance arriving on scene. The national targets specify that an ambulance should be on scene within eight minutes for 50% of incidents and within 14 minutes for 95% of cases. The impact of ALERT was assessed by comparing two month's figures: April 1994 and October 1994 (April was the only month prior to the implementation period for which adequate statistics were available).

At the 14-minute level, there was no noticeable change in performance (around 97% in both cases), but at the top end of the distribution there is, of course, much less scope for improvement. The presence of this "ceiling effect" argued for the use of the eight-minute index as a more sensitive indicator. Taking the eight-minute target, there was clear evidence of an improvement in performance with ALERT, with the "hit rate" increasing from 55.4% to 64.4%. This improvement is particularly impressive as the number of emergency incidents had increased by 15% between April and October, from a monthly total of 14,300 to 16,500. The reasons for this increase are beyond the scope of this article, suffice it to say that a number of factors were at work.

The Psychophysiological Dynamics of Despatching

The psychophysiological analysis focused exclusively on the work of the despatchers. Let us begin by noting that the despatcher's job is a critical and demanding one. In essence, despatching involves two interlinked tasks. The primary task involves identifying the location of an incident, prioritizing its importance, and finding the most appropriate ambulance to despatch. Linked to this is the complementary task of ensuring that there are no gaps in cover, i.e. local areas where all ambulances are active on jobs with none available for new emergencies. This secondary task can involve moving ambulances from one station to another, "like pieces on a chess board" as one despatcher put it. The essence of the despatcher's job is to balance these two tasks, in the stressful knowledge that life or death can depend on the decisions made. To compound matters, there is little spare capacity in the Service; for much of the working day, 50% of ambulances may be committed on jobs, with the figure rising as high as 80% at peak times. This combination of "cognitive complexity" and high risk in an uncertain, dynamic environment means that the work of the despatcher is inherently highly stressful.

In order to examine the relationship between blood pressure, subjective state, and workload, the data for each despatcher was inspected and two observation points were extracted: the time at which the despatcher was least heavily loaded and the time at which they were under the greatest pressure (workload was measured as the number of simultaneously active jobs). In order to obtain a satisfactory separation of high and low workload conditions, data was only used for those subjects whose maximum recorded workload was at least twice their minimum level.

Figure 1 shows the relationship between systolic blood pressure (SBP), heart rate (HR), and workload. (It will be noted that workload for ALERT peaks at a higher level than the pre-ALERT maximum, a further reflection of the general increase in demands that was noted earlier.) Both SBP and HR exhibit an increase with workload for paper-based and computer-supported conditions, although these trends were only significant for SBP ($F = 42.2$, $P < 0.001$; $F = 5.3$, $P < 0.05$). Although not shown, diastolic blood pressure also increased significantly with workload for both conditions ($F = 12.9$, $P < 0.001$, $F = 6.8$, $P < 0.01$). No overall differences

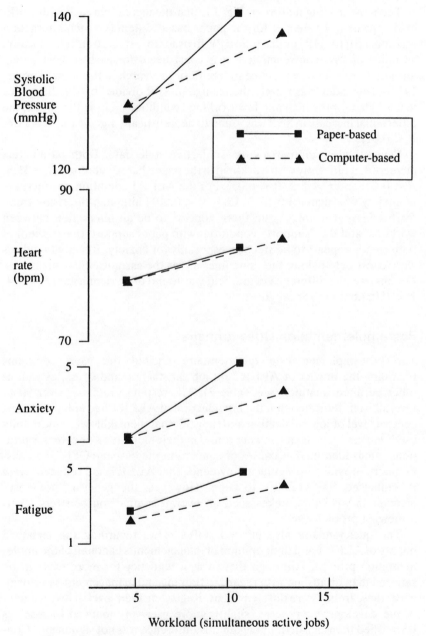

FIG. 1. Cardiovascular and subjective parameters as a function of workload.

(main effects) were significant for blood pressure or heart rate when comparing ALERT with the paper-based system.

The most striking feature of Fig. 1 is that the increase in SBP with workload appears to be steeper for the paper-based system (no such interaction was apparent for HR, or diastolic BP). In order to test this trend statistically, an index of "systolic reactivity" was constructed for each subject, along lines that are common practice in laboratory research in this area (Turner, 1994). This index was simply the change in SBP divided by the difference in workload for the high and low workload conditions. Using this index, the differential increase in SBP was found to be statistically significant ($F = 11.6$, $P < 0.01$).

Figure 1 also summarizes the subjective state data. Both parameters increased significantly with workload in the paper-based condition ($F = 31.6$, $P < 0.001$ and $F = 5.2$, $P < 0.05$). For the ALERT condition, the increase in anxiety was significant ($F = 18.5$, $P < 0.001$) although the rising trend for tiredness was not. Again there appears to be an interaction between workload and the "support" condition: with paper support, the gradient of both trends appears to be steeper, especially for anxiety. Reactivity indices were constructed along the same lines as for the cardiovascular measures. For anxiety, the difference in gradient was found to be significant ($F = 5.4$, $P < 0.05$) but not for fatigue.

Post-implementation Questionnaire

The post-implementation questionnaire elicited the users' opinions regarding the impact of ALERT on job satisfaction and stress, as well as other pertinent matters (see Table 2). The response rate was over 90%. Overall, staff indicated that the introduction of ALERT had enhanced their general level of job satisfaction and they felt that their skills were more fully used. However, no changes were found in their motivation or career aspirations, areas identified as causes of concern in the baseline OSI. The questionnaire provided no significant evidence that ALERT had reduced stress or enhanced staff's ability to cope. However, the general "pre–post" increase in workload makes such an overall comparison of stress levels somewhat problematic.

The questionnaire also elicited staff's views regarding the technical quality of ALERT and their opinion of management's handling of the implementation process. Although there was a tendency for more users to be satisfied than disatisfied with regard to training and management's performance, these trends were not significant. Regarding their level of involvement in the development process, slightly more users pronounced themselves dissatisfied than satisfied, but again this difference was not significant. Concerning the usability and effectiveness of the system, there were significantly more positive than negative ratings, i.e. users felt that the system was both easy to use and helped them do their job better. When asked if they would prefer to return to the paper system only 8% said they would; the over-whelming majority (83%) felt that ALERT represented a significant improvement over the paper system.

DISCUSSION

In contrast to many IT initiatives, the GMAS project appears to have been a success. The new computer system has been running smoothly now for over a year: there has been little evidence of user resistance, the system is manifestly well-liked by operators, and there are strong indications that service has improved. The new system is also associated with improved job satisfaction and objectively demonstrated reductions in operational stress levels. The latter is a particularly pleasing result as computerization is all too often linked to deleterious changes in working conditions (Briner & Hockey, 1988). The success of the project is all the more striking when compared to the failure in London. It is therefore pertinent to contrast the two cases in order to identify the critical factors in the Manchester project that were responsible for its success.

There appear to be two general areas where the London and Manchester experiences differ decisively, namely the management of the innovation process and the system design philosophy. Regarding the former, there is wide agreement in the research literature that two ingredients are critical to the success of IT projects: user involvement and management commit-ment (Wastell & Sewards, 1995). Whilst not a panacea, user involvement contributes vitally to the success of an IT project, both at a technical level by ensuring that design work is properly carried out, and at a psychological level by helping to foster a feeling of "ownership" by all stakeholders. The LAS project was conspicuously weak in this area, a general reflection of the poor state of industrial relations in LAS, and, in particular, management's lack of trust in the workforce. The official report (Page et al., 1993) observes that there was very little staff involvement in their computer project: as a result "there was no evidence of the staff having joint ownership of the system as one of the key stakeholders".

In comparison, GMAS management saw "ownership" as critical, and care was taken to involve the end-users in system development, as far as possible. Training was also given a high priority and considerable effort was put into the design of courses and other training material; this contrasts sharply with the situation in LAS where training was criticized both for its timing (too early) and quality (Page et al., 1993). Communication with staff was also given high priority by GMAS. Wastell and Newman (1993) have argued that the process of systems development is highly stressful: new systems entail turbulence and uncertainty; work practices, even employment itself, can be seen as under threat. GMAS's policy of openness and staff involvement meant that such anxieties were kept within bounds, and positive attitudes towards the system were maintained throughout.

Management commitment is another crucial success factor. There is no avoiding the responsibility on managers to play a leading role in overseeing the development of new systems. Should managers abdicate this role, the the prognosis for an IT project (indeed, any project) is poor (Laudon & Laudon, 1991; Lucas, 1981). In the London project, management commitment was lamentably weak. Project management was virtually non-existent (Page et al., 1993); no one from the service was assigned to work full time on the project and, by default, the system suppliers were left to manage progress themselves. In GMAS, by comparison, we have a model example of decisive leadership being exercised by the user side. The project manager was assigned full time to the project. He was well versed in computer technology and thus able to direct the project from a technical point of view. He was also a highly effective people-manager who worked with impressive attention to detail on the human side of the implementation process (training, communication, etc.).

At a more technical level there also appeared to be a fundamental difference between the two projects, namely in design philosophy. Kidd (1988) contends that the dominant paradigm of systems design is based on a "production machine" metaphor in which the underlying rationale is to replace, through automation, unreliable human labour by an infallible machine. In a simlar vein, Clegg et al. (1994) have argued that the majority of organizations follow a Tayloristic "task technology" approach to computerization (Blackler & Brown, 1986) which marginalizes the role of human and social factors (Clegg et al., 1994). In contrast, Kidd expounds an alternative design rationale (the "tool paradigm") in which the computer is seen as a prosthesis, a means of supporting and augmenting, not supplanting, the human user. The tool paradigm broadly corresponds with Blackler and Brown's "organization and end-user" design perspective, and reflects the sort of human-centred paradigm which is associated with Scandinavian design traditions (Ehn, 1988).

In many ways, the LAS project typifies the worst excesses of the automation approach. It was clear from the Inquiry's report (Page et al., 1993) that management saw the computer system as a device for exerting greater control over an undisciplined and inefficient workforce by imposing standardized and optimal procedures (e.g. over the choice of ambulance to mobilize). This sort of "Procrustean" approach is seen in many IT projects and is equally often the source of many of the troubles that beset such endeavours. Overly prescriptive and rigid systems undermine autonomy and create extra workload as users are forced to "work around" the inflexibilities of the system (Wastell, White, & Kawasek, 1994), thus engendering decrements not enhancements in productivity.

In the GMAS project there were the same temptations to automate many key aspects of the process. However, it is highly significant that such prescriptiveness was eschewed. In essence, the design philosophy of ALERT followed, albeit in an intuitive way, Kidd's (1988) tool paradigm. There was no question of the computer system usurping the human role. Through supportive information displays and the removal of unskilled secondary work (e.g. transcribing messages), ALERT was designed to support operators in their primary task of despatching ambulances. By deliberate design, ALERT did not encroach on the problem-solving kernel of the operator's job: the "nearest response sets", for instance, were for information only; decision making remained absolutely the prerogative of the operator.

The psychophysiological results provide a cogent demonstration of the benefits to be gained by designing systems to support human users. The results show that, whereas rising work demands evoke a "stress response" for both paper-based and computerized operation, the magnitude of the response (both in terms of subjective anxiety and objective physiological measures) was significantly lower for the computer-based system. The physiological results are particularly noteworthy. As noted earlier, cardiovascular mobilization is a central feature of the "active coping" response to a threat or challenge. In the case of a "cognitive challenge" this response is, of course, largely inappropriate, in the sense that vigorous physical activity is not usually entailed. None the less, cardiac mobilization occurs, of a magnitude commensurate with the degree of perceived threat. Increases in both heart rate and "pump force" (myocardial contractility) are involved, the latter reflected by elevated SBP (in contrast to diastolic BP which primarily reflects peripheral resistance to blood flow). Laboratory tasks have confirmed a relationship between task demands and both HR and SBP (Turner, 1994; Wright & Dill, 1993). The present results thus strongly suggest that rising task demands were experienced as less threatening with the support of ALERT; hence a less extreme stress response was evoked.

We may attribute this to the greater feeling of control endowed by the computer system. Control is a key factor mediating the relationship between stressors and their psychophysiological consequences; high levels of control enable individuals to cope with stress, low levels are associated with helplessness and strain (Karasek, 1979; Turner & Karasek, 1984). The support provided by ALERT allowed operators to concentrate their "cognitive resources" more effectively on their main task. It thus enabled a greater degree of control over a complex process with the result that stress levels were reduced, especially when work pressures were at their most acute. In part, this enhanced feeling of control was an objective reflection of increased competence (arising from the technical support provided by ALERT) but it is likely that support at a purely psychological level was also a factor (i.e. subjective feelings of security and shared responsibility arising from the presence of a tried and tested "electronic partner").

At this point, the limitations of the present study should be acknowledged. It is based on a single field study. Whilst such studies are rich in detail and high in external validity, the inherent weakness of control over events and circumstances inevitably threatens internal validity. Over the six months of the study, what else changed in the environment that might provide another explanation for our findings? There were certainly some significant changes (e.g. a redecoration of the control room) and Hawthorne effects must also be taken seriously. However, it is hard to see how such generalized changes could have produced the quite precise effects that were found here, namely a reduction in the slope of the relationship between work demands and stress levels. The most parsimonious explanation for this distinctive finding is that it was due to the introduction of the computer system.

In conclusion, the present study indicates that, despite the problematic nature of IT projects, the prognosis for such undertakings can be much improved by careful management of the innovation process, and by founding design on a tool paradigm, which emphasizes supporting and enhancing the human role, not supplanting it. Conventional systems development methods focus almost exclusively on technical issues (Kendall & Kendall, 1993); few methods pay explicit attention to human and organizational factors and those that do (e.g. ETHICS) are seldom seen in practice (Clegg et al., 1994). This is to be regretted as the present study provides compelling evidence that systems design based on human-centred principles can achieve not only enhancements in well-being, but also improved efficiency. Although an explicit methodology was not used, the success of the GMAS project thus supports the argument for the greater use of human-centred methods (Parker & Wall, 1995; Rosenbrock, 1989).

The adoption of a psychophysiological methodology was a key feature of the GMAS study. The hallmark of the psychophysiological approach is its real-time, "multimethod" character. These features are well-exemplified in the study where the real-time analysis of performance, physiology, and subjective state provided powerful convergent evidence that the new system had tangibly reduced stress levels. A number of writers have argued that psychophysiology has a valuable contribution to make to the design and evaluation of IT systems (Gale & Christie, 1987; Mullins & Treu, 1991; Nelson & Kletke, 1990; Wastell & Newman, 1993), especially in highly demanding environments where stress is a key issue. Psychophysiological techniques clearly have a particularly useful role to play in conjunction with methodologies such as sociotechnical systems design (Mumford, 1986) that aim at improvements in working conditions as well as efficiency gains. The present study has demonstrated the feasibility of the psychophysiological approach in a methodologically demanding field setting.

REFERENCES

Blackler, F., & Brown, C.A. (1986). Alternative models to guide the design and introduction of new information technologies into work organisations. *Journal of Occupational Psychology, 59*, 287–313.

Bramwell, R., & Cooper, C.L. (1995). VDUs in the workplace: Psychological and health implications. *International Review of Industrial and Organizational Psychology, 10*, 213–227.

Briner, R., & Hockey, G.R.J. (1988). Operator stress and computer-based work. In C.L. Cooper & R. Payne (Eds.), *Causes, coping and consequences of stress at work*. New York: Wiley.

Brown, I.D., Wastell, D.G., & Copeman, A. (1982). A psychophysiological investigation of system efficiency in public telephone systems. *Ergonomics, 25*, 1013–1040.

Clegg, C., Waterson, P. & Carey, N. (1994). Computer-supported collaborative working: Lessons from elsewhere. *Journal of Information Technology, 9*, 85–98.

Cooper, C.L., Sloan, S.J., & Williams, S. (1988). *The occupational stress indicator*. Windsor, UK: NFER-Nelson.

Ehn, P. (1988). *Work-oriented design of computer artifacts*. Stockholm, Sweden: Arbetsliv-centrum.

Frese, M. (1987a). A theory of control and complexity: Implications for software design and integration of computer systems into the workplace. In M. Frese, E. Ulich, & W. Dzida (Eds.), *Psychological issues of human–computer interaction in the workplace*. Amsterdam: North-Holland.

Frese, M. (1987b). Human computer interaction in the office. *International Review of Industrial and Organisational Psychology, 2*, 117–165.

Gale, A., & Christie, B. (1987). *Psychophysiology and the electronic workplace*. New York: Wiley.

Gladden, G. (1982). Stop the life-cycle: I want to get off. *Software Engineering Notes, 7*, 35–39.

Hacker, W. (1987). Computerisation versus computer aided mental work. In M. Frese, E. Ulich, & W. Dzida (Eds.), *Psychological issues of human–computer interaction in the workplace*. Amsterdam: North-Holland.

Hirschheim, R.A. (1985). *Office automation: A social and organisational perspective*. New York: Wiley.

Johansson, G., & Aronsson, G. (1984). Stress reactions in computerized administrative work. *Journal of Occupational Behaviour, 5*, 159–181.

Kahn, H.K., & Cooper, C.L. (1986). Computing stress. *Current Psychological Research and Reviews*, 148–162.

Karasek, R. (1979). Job demands, decision latitude and mental strain. *Administrative Science Quarterly, 24*, 285–307.

Kendall, J.E., & Kendall, K.E. (1993). Metaphors and methodologies: Living beyond the systems machine. *MIS Quarterly, 17*, 149–171.

Kidd, P. (1988). The social shaping of technology: The case of the CNC lathe. *Behaviour and Information Technology, 7*, 193–204.

Kuhmann, W. (1989). Experimental investigation of the stress-inducing properties of system response times. *Ergonomics, 32*, 271–280.

Laudon, K.C., & Laudon, J.P. (1991). *Management information systems: A contemporary perspective*. New York: Macmillan.

Light, K.C., Obrist, P.A., & Cubeddu, L.X. (1988). Evaluation of a new ambulatory blood pressure monitor (Accutracker 102): Laboratory comparisons with direct arterial pressure, stethoscope auscultatory pressure, and readings from a similar monitor. *Psychophysiology, 25*, 107–116.

Lucas, H. (1981). *Implementation: The key to successful information systems*. New York: Columbia University Press.

Lyytinen, K. (1988). Stakeholders, information systems failures and soft systems methodology. *Journal of Applied Systems Analysis, 15*, 61–81.

Mullins, P.M., & Treu, S. (1991). Measurement of stress to gauge user satisfaction with features of the computer interface. *Behavior and Information Technology, 10*, 325–343.

Mumford, E. (1986). *Using computers for business success: The ETHICS method*. Manchester, UK: Manchester Business School Press.

Nelson, D.L., & Kletke, M.G. (1990). Individual adjustment during technological innovation: A research framework. *Behaviour and Information Technology, 9*, 257–271.

Obrist, P.A. (1981). *Cardiovascular psychophysiology: A perspective*. London: Plenum Press.

Page, D., Williams, P., & Boyd, D. (1993). *Report of the inquiry into the London Ambulance Service*. Report commissioned by South West Thames Regional Health Authority, 40 Eastbourne Terrace, London, W2 3QR, UK.

Parker, S.K., & Wall, T.D. (1995). Job design and manufacturing. In P.B. Warr (Ed.), *Psychology at work*. London: Penguin Books.

Patrickson, M. (1986). Adaptation by employees to new technology. *British Psychological Society Journal, 59*, 1–11.

Rees, D.W., & Cooper, C.L. (1991). A criterion oriented validation study of the OSI outcome measures on a sample of health service employees. *Stress Medicine, 7*, 125–127.

Robertson, I.T., Cooper, C., & Williams, J. (1990). The validity of the occupational stress indicator. *Work and Stress, 4*, 29–39.

Rosenbrock, H.H. (1989). *Designing human-centred technology*. London: Springer-Verlag.

Sauer, C. (1993). *Why information systems fail: A case study approach*. Henley-on-Thames, UK: Waller.

Sundelin, G., & Hagberg, M. (1989). The effects of different pause types on neck and shoulder EMG activity during VDU work. *Ergonomics, 32*, 527–537.

Turner, J.A., & Karasek, R. (1984). Software ergonomics: Effects of computer application design parameters on operator task performance and health. *Ergonomics, 27*, 663–690.

Turner, J.R. (1994). *Cardiovascular reactivity and stress*. New York: Plenum Press.

Warr, P. (1987). *Psychology at work*. Harmondsworth, UK: Penguin.

Wastell, D.G. (1990). Mental effort and task performance: Towards a psychophysiology of human computer interaction. In D. Diaper (Ed.), *Proceedings of INTERACT 90*, Amsterdam, The Netherlands: Elsevier.

Wastell, D.G., Brown, I.D., & Copeman, A.K. (1982). Differential effects of workload on system performance in cord and cordless public telephone switchrooms. *Ergonomics, 25*, 1041–1052.

Wastell, D.G., & Newman, N. (1993). The behavioral dynamics of information system development: A stress perspective. *Accounting, Management and Information Technology, 3*, 121–148.

Wastell, D.G., & Sewards, A. (1995). An information systems profile of the UK manufacturing sector. *Journal of Information Technology, 10*, 179–189.

Wastell, D.G., White, P., & Kawalek, P. (1994). A methodology for business process redesign: Experiences and issues. *Journal of Strategic Information Systems, 3*, 23–40.

Wright, R.A., & Dill, J.C. (1993). Blood pressure responses and incentive appraisals as a function of perceived ability and objective task demand. *Psychophysiology, 30*, 152–160.

Zapf, D. (1993). Stress-oriented job analysis of computerised office work. *The European Work and Organizational Psychologist, 3*, 85–100.

Zuboff, S. (1982). New worlds of computer-mediated work. *Harvard Business Review, September*, 142–152.

EUROPEAN JOURNAL OF WORK AND ORGANIZATIONAL PSYCHOLOGY, 1996, 5 (3), 399–420

Representing Socio-technical Systems Options in the Development of New Forms of Work Organization

Ken Eason, Susan Harker, and Wendy Olphert

HUSAT Research Institute, Loughborough University, Loughborough, UK

It is widely accepted that effective implementation of new technology into work organizations needs an integrative approach in which developments in both technical and social systems are considered. Furthermore, success depends upon the effective participation of significant stakeholders in this process. This article reviews the methods available for this purpose and concludes that a particular weakness is the methods that can be used to generate and review socio-technical system opportunities early in the development process. Whilst methods exist to support stakeholder participation at this stage, they need to represent future socio-technical opportunities if they are to make an effective contribution. This article presents the ORDIT (Organizational Requirements Definition for Information Technology Systems) methodology, which uses responsibility modelling as a basis for constructing socio-technical systems opportunities. The application of telemedicine in health care is presented as a case study to demonstrate how this method can be used to construct and evaluate socio-technical scenarios.

THE OPPORTUNITY

New forms of information and communication technology offer enormous potential for the creation of new forms of work organization. These technologies can be used to change a face-to-face team working on a single site into a "virtual organization" in which the members work from a variety of sites, at home, or in vehicles, and communicate via the technology. The same technologies can be used to facilitate moves to flat, "networked" organizations (Savage, 1990) with open channels of communication between all members. They can, by contrast, be used as a means of monitoring and controlling staff within tightly controlled, centralized structures and can produce paced and deskilled jobs. In other applications a powerful personal computer, with access to a network, can be a sophistic-ated work tool and can empower knowledge workers to develop their

Requests for reprints should be addressed to K. Eason, HUSAT Research Insititute, Loughborough University, Loughborough LE11 3TU, UK.

competencies to the full. The technology can also provide a rich medium of communication and control across organizational boundaries and can therefore be used to "outsource" activities or have them undertaken "off-shore", e.g. in a third-world country where labour costs are low. Advances in automation make it possible to "downsize". All these factors enhance the possibility of "casualization" and of using contract labour rather then permanent staff.

Such potential creates powerful forces for change in an organization. Different "stakeholders" (Mitroff, 1980), i.e. people with a stake in the current situation and in the consequences of any change, will take different views of the desirability of these changes. The technology is immensely flexible and it can be used to facilitate a wide variety of organizational forms. There is an opportunity for stakeholders in a particular organization to seek ways of capitalizing on these possibilities and find a new form of work organization that enhances their collective work objectives and meets many of their personal needs. The purpose of this article is to explore the approaches that are available to represent future socio-technical options, and to help stakeholders choose between them. The next section summarizes the problems we have to address, and the subsequent three sections present currently available methods of solving the problem. The penultimate two sections introduce the ORDIT methodology—a new approach we have created to fill the need for methods that can serve participative design objectives early in the development process. In the final section we present our conclusions.

THE PROBLEM

Over 10 years of experience of applying new technology within organizations allows a number of conclusions to be drawn.

1. The failure rate of major applications of information technology in organizations is high: Lyytinen and Hirschheim (1987), for example, claim that more than 50% end in failure and that the primary cause of failure is lack of attention to significant organizational issues.

2. The reason no attention is paid to organizational issues is that these developments are usually conceived as technical innovations for specific business purposes. It is often assumed that there will be no organizational change. In practice, however, the technology produces knock-on effects in the organization with unintended and often negative outcomes. There are many examples where the members of the organization have reacted against the technical system and it has been rejected. The very public failure of a computer despatch system for the London Ambulance Service (Page, Williams, & Boyd, 1993) is a case in point where a technical solution made

it very difficult for staff to undertake their duties effectively, with the result that patients waited many hours for an ambulance. Finally, the system was scrapped and a complete redesign undertaken.

3. In situations where organizational change is intended, it is often assumed that the introduction of the system will automatically achieve it. It may be expected that reduction and consequent savings in labour will be directly achieved from the extra efficiency of the technical system. Or, for example, factories may be conceived as automated plants requiring a small number of people with specialist skills, while in practice it is found that many diverse human skills are still required. Failure to address the need for planned reorganization leads to an *ad hoc*, "plug the gaps" approach after implementation, and rarely creates an optimal structure as a result.

4. There is the situation where technical systems are constructed after a business analysis has been undertaken, for example in the form of business process re-engineering (Hammer & Champy, 1990). In this case, a fuller understanding of the relationship between the business and technical system will be developed. The result is usually a substantial change in the organization but the effect of driving the initiative on the basis of business and technical criteria is often that little attention is paid to the human implications. As a result many of these innovations run into difficulty because the significance of the human contribution has been overlooked in the planning.

One way of summarizing the process that underpins these conclusions is to depict the changes in two parts (Eason, 1996a): (1) the formal, planned design and development process—in most applications this is focused on business and technical issues; (2) the informal and unplanned phase, when members of the organization begin to appreciate the consequences of the new system—they may find they have to adapt to the new situation, often in dysfunctional and stressful ways, and they may react by rejecting or marginalizing the technical system. Eason (1996a) provides nine case examples of this two-stage process. In most of the cases the formal agenda of the initial design process paid very little attention to organizational implications and possibilities, with the consequence that these emerged in unplanned ways after implementation. The absence of a systematic approach to the planning of organizational change is supported by a survey of 55 organizations implementing new technology, undertaken by Docherty and King (1995). Fifty-four percent of the sample made no attempt to treat organizational issues formally and, even when they were recognized as important, the technical staff leading the change process felt it was the responsibility of others to deal with these issues.

Walton (1989), conducting a secondary analysis of 19 cases of new system implementation, identified three critical success factors associated with successful implementation:

1. The formal design agenda was to develop an integrated system in which equal attention was paid to the business goals and processes and the technical and social systems that provided the resources to accomplish the business goals.
2. All the stakeholders in the organization participated in the development process both to provide their expertise and to develop a commitment to the chosen solution.
3. All the users developed a mastery of the technology so that they could exploit the potential for meeting business goals.

Whilst Walton gives examples where all these factors have been present and success was achieved, he also has examples where failure resulted from inattention to these factors. His study focuses attention on the need to find ways of systematically addressing human, business, and technical considerations in the development of integrated systems to serve the full range of organizational needs. The development of methods which can achieve these goals is therefore important and such methods must incorporate techniques which allow the major stakeholders within the organization both to contribute their knowledge of the human and social issues and to promote their ownership of the integrated system that emerges.

METHODS FOR INTEGRATED SYSTEMS DESIGN

As a result of working with many organizations to help them plan and implement integrated systems that do take both the human and social issues into account, the HUSAT Research Institute has used a wide range of methods to support this objective. One conclusion we reached is that, whilst there are numerous methods available to help the technical analyst and designer, there is a paucity of methods to help in the creation of integrated solutions. The purpose of this article is to discuss the methods that are available, to comment on their strengths and weaknesses, and to present the ORDIT methodology (Organizational Requirements Definition for Information Technology Systems), which supports the development of integrated systems by taking full account of human, social, and organizational requirements.

In evaluating the available methods for these purposes, the analysis in the previous section suggests that the following criteria have to be satisfied:

1. A method must help the process of reviewing the organizational implications of technical systems and of new business processes. Ideally it should facilitate the determination of business and technical implications of new forms of work organization. In short, the method needs to facilitate easy movement between the three domains of discourse (business, technical, and organizational) that make up the integrated work system.

2. A method must facilitate the articulation of a variety of options for the future integrated system, the articulation of criteria for the assessment of options, and for the selection of viable ways forward. The great benefit of modern technology is its flexibility, and to exploit this it is necessary to assess alternative ways of using it.

3. A method must support the engagement of a wide range of participants in the development process. It must help domain specialists contribute their specialist knowledge (business, technical, and organizational) and above all it must support the stakeholders in the organization to express their expertise and to examine the degree to which different options for the future meet their requirements. (Throughout this article we refer to stakeholder rather than user participation because there may be a wider population of interested parties in an organization than the potential users. Stakeholders therefore subsume all potential users.)

In the next section we consider some existing methods against these criteria.

A CLASSIFICATION OF EXISTING METHODS FOR INTEGRATED DESIGN

A simple matrix is produced in Fig. 1 classifying the different types of method that have been used to support the development of integrated systems along three dimensions that have significant implications for the way in which methods are used.

The first important dimension concerns the type of contribution the method makes to the development process. Some methods involve the construction and representation of solutions to the design problem (Solution Content). Other methods concentrate upon the procedures for analysis, design, and evaluation that need to be followed to produce a solution (Design Process). A second dimension concerns the level of detail at which the method works. Some of the most popular methods apply at the level of an individual user working with equipment (Human–machine Systems), whilst others apply at the broader level where the social system interacts with the technical system (Socio-technical Systems). A third dimension concerns the time at which the method can be applied. Some methods can be used early in the development process (Early); others are most useful close to the point of implementation (Late).

A number of methods have been positioned in relation to the three dimensions in Fig. 1 to illustrate the variations that are possible. While the examples do not constitute a comprehensive set, they all share the property that they can be used in circumstances where the development involves crossing boundaries between business needs, technical opportunities, and organizational change. We will begin by reviewing methods available at late stages in system development.

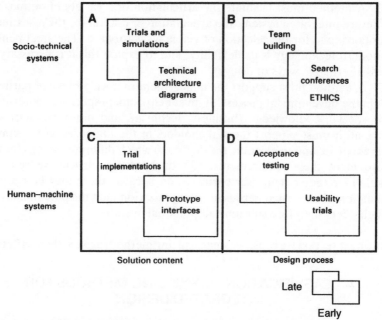

FIG. 1. Methods to support the design of integrated systems.

When a technical system is at a point of development where it can be tried in an operational environment, integrated design can be accomplished by direct examination of the human and organizational consequences that result. In category C at the human–machine system level, for example, trial workstations can be installed and (in category D) acceptance tests can be undertaken. The same is true at the socio-technical systems level. An operational version of the system makes it possible to mount trials and simulations (category A) to test it in its organizational context. The extensive set of methods in category B, created by organizational development specialists to facilitate organizational change, for example, team building, is relevant to the process of adoption of the new system. The great advantage of all these approaches is that the real system is available to assess implications. The great disadvantage is that, if the assessment reveals problems, it may be too late to make major changes in the technical system because the investment has been made. A common outcome of these approaches is that they are used to help the organization assimilate the changes caused by the technical system.

If the examination of human and organizational issues is to have real influence over the design of the technical system, the examination must take place early in the development process before technical investments are made. In recent years considerable strides have been made in methods to accomplish early influences at the human–machine systems level. In category C the popular method is to create a prototype of the technical form of interaction which users can work with at an early stage of design. This has long been the practice in ergonomics where early mock-ups of future workstations have been created to evaluate the implications for the human operator. With the advent of rapid prototyping languages it is now possible to create very realistic software interfaces, which would-be users can interact with to examine how tasks will be undertaken (Harker, 1991). The complement to such representation of future systems is the development of usability evaluation procedures, such as those identified in category D (see, for example, Andriessen, 1995; Preece, 1994), which provide a variety of methods for assessing whether users can use proposed systems effectively, efficiently, and with satisfaction. These methods make it possible to improve the usability of the technical system before it is implemented.

The position at the socio-technical systems level is not so advanced. There are many methods in category B developed by organizational development (OD) specialists that support stakeholders in the review of future organizational options. Search conferences (Weisbord, 1990) and ETHICS (Mumford, 1983a, 1983b) provide, for example, processes for stakeholders to analyse future needs, understand the current position, and develop a plan for moving from the present to the future desired state. These methods do not, however, provide detailed techniques for representing future socio-technical system opportunities and they are not the methods commonly used in the development of information technology systems. The most common way of representing future systems proposals at an early stage in development (category A) is to prepare flow charts which use technical terminology to represent how the future technical system will function (Smith, 1993). The process of using these to assess organizational implications involves user representatives reviewing the technical descriptions to detect and evaluate the organizational effects. There is strong evidence (Hornby & Clegg, 1992) that users experience great difficulty both in understanding the technical description and in assessing the organizational implications.

TRIALS AND SIMULATIONS USED EARLY IN DESIGN

Our review of existing approaches suggests that the greatest need is for methods at the socio-technical level that facilitate early integrated design. Of the methods described in the previous section, trials or simulations of operational systems in organizational contexts provide the best evidence of organizational impact. Unfortunately they are often conducted too late in the development process to influence the design of the technical system. It is possible to use these methods at an early stage of development and we have had several opportunities to try this approach. We now give three examples, which are presented in order to assess what can be done at an early stage and to explicate the advantages and disadvantages of this approach to the goal of integrated design.

A Mobile Communications System Trial

An electricity company wished to improve communications between the enquiry desk, which customers rang to request services, and the electricians in the field, who were responsible for dealing with the service requests. The radio provided in the electrician's van was inadequate when the electrician was with a customer, requiring repeated attempts to contact the relevant electrician. The company selected a data transmission system that enabled the clerks on the enquiry desks to send data to a receiver in each van. This could store up to 25 messages, which could be sent at any time irrespective of whether the electrician was present or not. A pilot trial of the system was run in one of the company's regions. This was a live operational trial and the system was used as the major way of allocating work. The technical system worked well but the users quickly identified several serious organizational problems. The electricians found that because new work could arrive at any time it became impossible for them to plan their day. The local foreman, who was responsible for all the electricians, no longer knew what work had been assigned to his staff, and the clerks, at the centre, were being asked to make decisions about the allocation of service jobs without understanding the nature of the job or the local geography, both of which the electricians used to plan their day's work. These problems led to the withdrawal of the trial system and the company began to reconsider the kind of system that would be required both to speed the process of allocating work and to enable the electricians and foreman to utilize their specialist knowledge. A fuller account of this case is given in Eason (1996b).

Organizational Prototyping in Freight Forwarding

A national freightforwarding company had branches in all major cities and ports in the country. It wished to implement information technology in each branch in order that consignment details need only be captured once and could then be used to generate shipping orders, customs clearance, insurance, billing, etc. The company also wished to explore whether the system could be used for the consolidation of loads, i.e. collecting part loads from neighbouring cities for transport to a particular port. A cheap "off-the-shelf" version of a system, which would support this task, was purchased and introduced for an operational test in three neighbouring branches. Despite some inadequacies in the off-the-shelf system, it demonstrated to staff the value of using such an approach to manage the wide variety of form-filling tasks needed for each consignment. But they found it much less successful in supporting the task of consolidating loads. The branch managers encountered many problems in agreeing with colleagues in other branches; for example, there were issues about who took the lead, how to share the payment, whose load had priority, etc. The branches had previously been entirely autonomous and the significant organizational change associated with the requirement to co-operate was seen as a major threat. When the full system was designed and implemented this feature was dropped. A fuller account is presented in Klein and Eason (1991).

A System for Payment Processing

A major organization providing payments as a result of insurance claims through a nationwide branch network was developing a large-scale computer system. At the same time, it was undergoing major organizational change as a result of the introduction of new policies. It wanted to explore new ways of organizing work in branches to achieve new performance objectives, and to assess whether the proposed computer system (which had been specified before the new policies came into effect) would support different kinds of job. Having identified an option that appeared to offer benefits in terms of operational efficiency and staff satisfaction, an experiment was set up to examine whether the proposed design of the new computer system would support this organizational option. A prototype of the proposed system was built, and a simulated branch office environment was set up in a laboratory. A sample of normal branch staff were asked to try out the new work organization, which involved taking data for a claim during an interview with role-playing "clients", and entering it onto the computer using the prototype system. The experiment showed that, while the work organization option was feasible, there were serious reservations about the way in which its proposed implementation in the technical system would affect the quality of the interaction with the client. In particular, it raised questions about the confidentiality of the information the clerk could call up on the screen, the extent to which the clerk and claimant should be able to share the information presented, and how privacy could be maintained. Changes were made in the detailed aspects of the way in which clerk and claimant worked together and the on-screen presentation of information from the database was changed before the system was implemented.

Strengths and Weaknesses

The strength of methods based on trials and simulations is that they enable stakeholders and users to see new technical systems in their organizational context and to work with them on real tasks. The form of representation of the new socio-technical system is real, dynamic, and concrete, especially where the trial is live. Even in the simulation everything was realistic except that the claimants received no money. It is a relatively easy task under these circumstances for staff to assess the usefulness of the technical system and to explore the organizational implications in the form of changes in relationships it might create. The data gathered is rich and the stakeholders are very well informed and able to make good judgements about how they wish the main systems development to proceed.

There are, however, considerable weaknesses. It is dangerous to use trials of this kind as evidence of the likely reaction of staff when the main system is implemented. This is an almost classical situation for the "Hawthorne effect" (Rothlisberger & Dickson, 1939). The spotlight is on the staff involved and they usually respond with interest and commitment. Tapscott (1982, p. 199) has captured the problem in his "second law of office systems: The ease of a pilot implementation is inversely related to the complexity of its operational extension". What is gained is an understanding of the adequacy of the technical system and its organizational implications. Another serious drawback is that it is difficult to set up and test alternative forms of socio-technical system in operational trials. Trials can be expensive to mount and monitor. As a result they tend to be used within the standard technically-dominated development process to examine the proposed solution, with little attention being paid to the range of socio-technical opportunities that may be available.

From this analysis we can identify a particular weakness in the array of methods available. What is lacking is a method which can be used early in the development process to enable stakeholders to explore possible socio-technical system opportunities and evaluate their consequences. To this we can add the pragmatic consideration that a method is needed that is cheap enough to gain widespread adoption. The method needs to make it possible for a range of options to be articulated early, in order that the stakeholders will have a chance to consider the directions they wish to support before the investment in a particular form of technical system takes place. Methods such as search conferences and ETHICS provide participative processes that can support this activity. The major gap lies in the availability of a way to create representations of future socio-technical systems which participants can use to explore organizational implications. The current practice of using technical representations does not support this analysis. In the next section we present the ORDIT methodology, which was developed to satisfy these criteria.

THE ORDIT METHODOLOGY

The ORDIT (Organizational Requirements Definition for Information Technology Systems) methodology was developed in response to a recognition that conventional methods for capturing the requirements for information technology systems focused upon business or functional needs and tended to overlook the many organizational requirements that affect the ultimate take-up of the system (Olphert & Harker, 1994). ORDIT was developed within the European Union ESPRIT programme by a consortium from the UK, Eire, and Italy and includes specialists in organizational behaviour and formal methods. This methodology was created by an iterative process, which used many realistic case studies to test the emerging methods. A description of the methodology follows, together with its rationale, and this is followed by two worked examples.

The initial task was to find a way of identifying at the beginning of the development process those organizational, social, and human needs that are not normally captured early in the process. The case studies demonstrated that these requirements belong to a wide range of organizational stakeholders. They could include overall policies of the organization, for example, to create a secure and reliable system or to preserve corporate identity; they could reflect sectional and individual needs, for example, for job security, privacy, and autonomy. It quickly became apparent that stakeholders were unable to identify those requirements that would be important without assistance. Whilst they might be able to make very general statements, they could not make them specific to requirements for a technical system because they could not see any association between the organizational issues and the nature of technical system being planned. An important conclusion drawn from this is that the term "requirements capture" commonly used in the systems development community, is not appropriate. The process is a far more active one and it has to be supported by methods of "requirements generation". The ORDIT methodology therefore provides a means to present stakeholders with socio-technical visions of the future including alternative solutions that (1) involve different organizational, business, and technical solutions, (2) can be evaluated from the different stakeholder perspectives, and (3) will generate requirements through a process of iteration.

The methodology consists of a modelling language that can be used to construct socio-technical visions and a participative process that enables stakeholders gradually to identify and refine their requirements. The modelling language had to be able to represent the business, technical, and organizational parts of the integrated system and it takes as its points of departure socio-technical systems theory (from organizational theory) and enterprise modelling (from formal approaches to requirements capture). Socio-technical systems theory (see Emery & Trist, 1969; Herbst, 1974) provides a means of representing the input, throughput, and output to a system within an open framework which produces variance for the system to handle. The work is undertaken by a network of work roles with each role supported by relevant tools and technology. Enterprise modelling

(Martin & Dobson, 1991) has developed similar concepts from a different perspective. In this case an enterprise undertakes its work through the actions of agents who need information to fulfil their responsibilities.

The ORDIT process for developing requirements for socio-technical system alternatives depicted in Fig. 2 has four interrelated activities. An initial scoping exercise determines several features of the process: (1) it defines the scope of the work system that may be subject to change, (2) it establishes the stakeholders who have an interest in the future of the work system, and (3) it establishes the nature of the contract between the stakeholders and those applying the ORDIT methodology. Following the scoping exercise, the stakeholders are helped to make an initial statement of their requirements for the changed situation. At this stage this would be expected to be a broad-brush statement of hopes and fears. In parallel, the existing work system is examined as a socio-technical system, and an enterprise model developed. The information gathered from the broad statement of requirements is then applied to the enterprise model to generate a number of future options which may have various organizational, business, and technical ramifications. A structured process for participative evaluation of the options then helps to detail, elaborate, and prioritize the requirements. Typically the presentation of different options stimulates the identification of different kinds of requirements and draws different degrees of support from different stakeholders. These options provide a basis for stakeholders to seek consensus about the requirements to be sought and to identify the option which provides the best opportunity to meet these requirements. The output of the ORDIT process is a specification for the

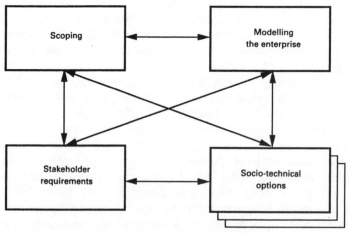

FIG. 2.   Activities in an ORDIT analysis. (Adapted from the *ORDIT process manual*, ORDIT Consortium, 1993.)

required technical system and a view of the social system towards which the organization will move. Figure 2 is depicted as four interacting but different activities because each leads to further work on the others. It is not a process statement, although scoping is inevitably the starting point and an agreed specification for a future socio-technical system is the output.

The enterprise modelling language which is used to model the existing work systems and to represent future options uses responsibility as its key concept. Figure 3 is a simplified ORDIT model using the example of a restaurant to illustrate the main features of this language. Responsibility provides an enduring bridge between the enterprise (or business) goals and process, the social system, and the technical system. To achieve enterprise goals requires a system in transaction with its environment, and one way of expressing what will have to be achieved is as a set of responsibilities—in

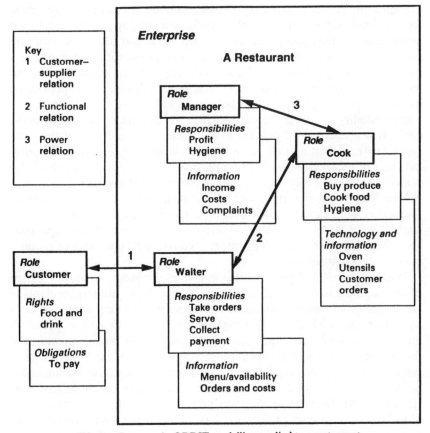

FIG. 3.   Concepts in ORDIT modelling applied to a restaurant.

the case of a restaurant for example, to offer food that is appetising, meet health regulations, offer safe and comfortable seating, etc.

The responsibilities are both functional, e.g. to cook the food, and non-functional, e.g. to provide a convivial environment. The business process will specify the activities necessary to move from inputs (food raw materials, customers at the door) to outputs (satisfied customers, bills paid, dishes washed) and the social system specifies the way of allocating the respons-ibilities to work roles. This provides a more enduring way of describing the social system than using task descriptions because responsibility describes what has to be achieved without specifying how it is achieved. Once the responsibilities have been allocated, the technical resources required can be determined, e.g. the cook needs the oven, the cooking utensils, etc., the waiter needs the menus, the order pads, etc. Some of the technical resources will be informational and the responsibilities will define these requirements and the rights and obligations the role holder will have to them. For example, the customer has a right to be informed about the charges made for the food that is ordered and an obligation to pay in response to the presentation of the appropriate information about that which has been con-sumed. It is possible to use the concept of responsibility in this way as a means of moving between the business description, the social system, and the technical system. It also has several other advantages. It provides a means of describing the relations between role holders, e.g. the waiter has a responsibility to take the customer's order and convey it accurately to the cook. It is also a way of expressing the underlying character of the work system without getting tied down by the specific ways in which respons-ibilities are handled in the existing system. It also provides the basis for describing different ways of engaging in the business process because these will imply different allocations of responsibilities and of technical resources. The waiter, for example, could collect the payment from customers or they could pay a cashier on exit. The restaurant may, for example, have specialist cooks and therefore a need for waiters to convey different kinds of require-ment to different cooks.

Within the ORDIT approach the modelling language provides a means of developing a variety of scenarios that reflect the future requirements of the major stakeholders. We could, for example, develop scenarios for a restaurant that wished to add a "take-away" service or go for special set meals at low prices, etc. Each scenario would display the main features of the business process, the allocation of responsibilities, and the technical support for each role. This kind of scenario provides a basis for the stake-holders to conduct what we have called a "user–cost benefit assessment" (Eason, 1988). In this process, stakeholders can examine the implications of the scenario for each of the work role holders. We have found it useful to provide a structure in which stakeholders first identify the likely changes in the role and then evaluate the extent to which these changes represent benefits or "costs" in the sense of disadvantages. Benefits and costs can be identified at a number of levels; on the tasks undertaken, the responsibilities in the work role, and the relations between roles and consequences for personnel issues such as job security, career opportunities, and reward systems. The evaluation helps stakeholders to identify the social system implications of each scenario and to specify in greater detail the requirements they wish to seek in future developments. A typical output of this process is that each scenario produces "winners" (who get mostly benefits) and "losers" (who get mostly costs). Since this is early in the development process there is an opportunity to search for solutions that give each stakeholder some significant benefit. Boehm, Bose, Horowitz, and Lee (1994), working within a similar framework, express this approach in terms of finding "win–win" outcomes, to which all stakeholders will commit themselves.

The focal point of this technique is the development of the alternative scenarios and the evaluation process. Eason and Olphert (1995) provide an example of this technique applied to the case study described earlier concerning the application of mobile communications in an electricity supply company. In order to illustrate this in more detail the next section provides a worked example in an application based in the health care sector.

A TELEMEDICINE EXAMPLE

An exciting potential application of information technology is telemedicine in which a doctor may examine and treat a patient at a distance by using multimedia communications to provide pictures and data, to allow verbal communication, etc. Application of this technology could achieve the following goals. Patients who are in remote places or cannot easily be transported to hospital could be given medical help. It could mean more patients could be treated in the community with a saving on hospital time and resources and savings in transport costs. Although there is wide recognition of the rich potential of this technology, there have as yet been few implementations and the complexity of the systems that would be introduced involve such significant social, economic, and technical challenges that it is important to evaluate alternative options before much further work is done. Now is an appropriate time to anticipate the socio-technical implications of deploying telemedicine applications. It is our belief that, even if the technology works effectively, there will be serious organizational issues, particularly affecting the allocation of responsibilities for medical care. We have accordingly been researching the organizational implications of a particular application of telemedicine using the ORDIT methodology. We have been assisted by health service staff, although these studies are currently only for research purposes rather than part of a specific development.

The envisaged application of telemedicine would support the provision of specialist health care, presently based in hospitals, to remote locations where both routine and emergency treatment could be provided.

A macro analysis of the existing work processes associated with primary and secondary health care identifies six significant stakeholder groups: patients, emergency services, primary care doctors (General Practitioners in the UK), medical specialists in hospitals, accident and emergency centres, and medical administrative authorities. The existing processes can be divided into routine referrals and emergency admissions. In the routine procedure the patient is first seen by the General Practitioner and, if the doctor feels the need for specialist advice, the patient is referred to a relevant specialist in a hospital, attends an out-patient clinic at the hospital, and may be admitted if the specialist considers it necessary. Responsibility for the patient then passes from the General Practitioner to the medical specialist. In the emergency situation rescue services, doctors, and others may provide temporary treatment where the emergency has occurred and then the patient is transported to the accident and emergency centre for further treatment. If necessary, the patient may then be admitted to a hospital ward under the care of a relevant medical specialist.

An ORDIT model, which identifies the responsibilities of each stakeholder group at each stage of the process, was constructed. Such a model can be constructed to a level of detail beyond the scope of this article. Examples of the kinds of information it yields are that only medically qualified staff have the right to prescribe treatments and they are under obligation to operate to the specific demands of a medical code of ethics. The staff involved will also have a responsibility for the effective and efficient use of medical resources and will be monitored by the medical administrative authorities.

This model was used to created two alternative scenarios of how telemedicine might be used in the future, first in the routine referral setting and second in the emergency. The initial scenarios were created by allocating features of the technology to work roles on the basis of early visions of how it might work.

Routine Referrals Model

Scenario 1 was for the routine referrals. This scenario was developed to show the process of using telemedicine, the allocation of the responsibilities of various work roles in the process, and the technical facilities available to each work role. The surgery of each General Practitioner would be equipped with a telemedicine facility which could be linked with a studio-based telemedicine facility in the nearest general hospital. When a GP considers that a hospital referral is appropriate and does not wish a patient to travel to the hospital an appointment can be made for a telemedicine consultation with an appropriate specialist at the hospital. On the appointed day the patient attends the GP's surgery and the GP creates the telemedicine link and acts as local assistant whilst the specialist makes an examination of the patient and makes a diagnosis. In the scenario, unless the specialist feels that every effort must be made to bring the patient to the hospital, the specialist advises the General Practitioner on treatment. Throughout this process the GP remains responsible for the patient and completes the records.

An evaluation of this scenario by means of the user cost–benefit assessment method from the perspectives of the major stakeholder groups revealed a number of significant issues. All agreed that the use of the technology was potentially beneficial in the treatment of patients and in savings on transport and hospital visits. However, all stakeholders also identified potential "costs". The patients were concerned about their privacy because it was not clear who would have access to the consultation at the hospital or what records would be retained. The GPs were concerned about the extent of their responsibility: For example, what would be the implications if they ignored the advice of the specialist if they felt it was inappropriate? They also felt that holding a conversation with the specialist about the patient's condition in the presence of the patient would create severe constraints on the communication. They were also concerned that they would be expected to maintain, understand, and operate in their surgeries sophisticated equipment with very little relevant expertise. The medical specialists were concerned that they might be asked to undertake a diagnosis that was difficult to make when mediated by the technology. They felt the GPs were determining the use of this form of consultation and they might not have the medical knowledge to do this appropriately. They were also concerned that records of the consultation would be kept and could be used to assess their competence in making the diagnosis. The Health Authority that was paying for the system was concerned that usage was under the control of the GPs and they could make inefficient use of the resource provided both locally and in the hospital.

This evaluation created a very considerable elaboration of the socio-technical system requirements for this telemedicine application to be used effectively. It led to questions about the social system, e.g. who is in control of initiating the consultation, subsequent treatment, etc., and how the privacy and interests of the patient are to be protected, and about the technical system at many levels, e.g. what information flows ahead of the consultation, what flows to the administrative authority, how is the system maintained and users supported, can the patient see the medical specialist as well as vice versa, can the doctors converse without the patient seeing or hearing, etc.?

Following the evaluation of scenario 1 it is possible to construct other scenarios to meet some or all of these requirements. Another scenario might place responsibility for establishing a telemedicine consultation with the hospital specialist. The GP could make a normal referral request and the specialist could determine whether this was an appropriate use of the technology. An evaluation of this scenario raises questions for the GP and the Health Authority about whether the specialist would be in possession of all the relevant information to make such decisions. A different kind of scenario would be to establish a telemedicine unit (probably at the hospital), which would act as the support for the technical facilities at the hospital and also in the surgeries of the GPs. It could also act as a training centre for all users. Evaluation of this scenario suggests it answers some needs but raises questions about whether training could be extended to cover medical questions about when it is appropriate to use these facilities and to control issues about the scheduling of scarce resources. Before looking at these issues it is useful to look at the implications of the scenario for handling emergency telemedicine consultations.

Emergencies Model

Scenario 2 dealt with the treatment of emergency cases. This scenario was developed, as before, to show the process of using telemedicine, the responsibilities of various work roles in the process, and the technical facilities available to each work role. In this scenario the emergency services (ambulance, air/sea rescue, mountain rescue, etc.) are provided with portable and robust telemedicine equipment. When they have a patient in distress who needs immediate medical attention they can use this equipment to get direct medical advice. GPs can also use their surgery facilities to obtain emergency specialist medical advice. The scenario envisages that, when an emergency requires this service, the people at the scene can call a relevant hospital specialist who can go to the telemedicine facility at the hospital, receive pictures of the patient, and discuss the patient's condition with the people on the spot.

This scenario was also evaluated using the user–cost benefit assessment method from the perspective of each of the stakeholders. Again it demonstrated a general view that this was a facility that could be of great benefit to patients who needed expert attention, for example before they could be moved. The rescue services and GPs felt it would give them a greater sense of security and confidence, and hospital staff felt that it would mean that patients would be in a better condition when they arrived at the hospital. Again each stakeholder had reservations. The rescue services were worried about taking care of sophisticated equipment in difficult circumstances and how long it would be before they could get expert help with questions about what they should do in the interim. The hospital staff were worried by this extension of their responsibility to be "on call" and were concerned that they should only be summoned when they were really needed. They were also concerned about the quality of information which would be available as the basis on which to offer advice and who would be responsible if misdiagnosis or mistreatment resulted from the poor quality of the communication. The administrative authority was also concerned that the facility was used only in circumstances when it was most needed and were concerned about the definition of such situations. The Accident and Emergency Department of the hospital felt that the absence of their involvement in the envisaged system created problems because, in most circumstances, the patient would later be brought to them in the hospital and if they were involved, they would be better informed and able to prepare to treat the patient. Furthermore, the medical staff in the Accident and Emergency Department wondered why they were not asked to give advice because they were more skilled in dealing with patients in emergency conditions than most medical specialists.

This evaluation also elaborated the social system requirements needed to use this facility effectively. In particular it raises questions about the training required in how to use equipment, when to use it, and who to call. Specifically, the evaluators questioned how rescuers would know which specialist to call in the emergency situation. An alternative scenario, which gained support from many stakeholders, was for the call to go to a telemedicine facility associated with the Accident and Emergency Department because they had experts in this kind of human condition. If the unit could also be staffed by people expert in the use of the equipment, it would provide all the support necessary. It was a short step to recognize that this unit might also serve the support needs for routine referrals. The scenario that is gaining support therefore is one in which a telemedicine unit is responsible for the facility and has a range of responsibilities including training, advice on circumstances in which it is of value, a responsibility for effective use of resources to the administrative authority, and care for ethical considerations in dealing with patients, etc. Such a proposal forms the basis on which a demonstration of telemedicine applications is developing in France through the mediation of their equivalent of the accident and emergency services.

This example demonstrates that early conceptions of how technology might operate in a work setting are often inadequate. There is a real danger that in a technology-dominated development process the inadequacies might not be revealed until implementation. Even if trials are run before implementation it may be difficult and expensive to make the changes necessary in the technology and the organization to develop an effective socio-technical system. The ORDIT method gives sufficient insight into possible socio-technical futures for the stakeholders to appreciate the implications very early in the process and to seek consensus about both the technical and the organizational way forward. At the same time, the stakeholders are participating in a meaningful and influential way in the development, which has the potential to gain their commitment to the system when it is implemented.

CONCLUSIONS

It is a truism to say that many applications of new technology have unfortunate and unplanned organizational implications, which may put people under stress, cause a rejection of the technology, etc. Our view is that we need methods to support participative and integrative systems development in order that organizational requirements and options are considered alongside technical opportunities. We have reviewed the methods available for integrative and user-centred work and we recognize several strengths. The methods available at the individual human–computer interface level provide ways of prototyping the future system early in development and of helping would-be users evaluate it for effectiveness, usability, acceptability, etc.

We are more concerned about the methods available at the socio-technical level of design. Here, we seem to be strong in methods we can use at the point of implementation in trials and simulations—but often this is too late to make major changes. Earlier in the development process, we have access to participative methods used, for example, in organizational development, but these are not strong in support of the close examination of the interaction between planned social systems and planned technical systems. Too often in development processes, user participation consists of asking users to review abstract technical description to judge the organizational implications.

The ORDIT methodology provides better support for user-centred integrative analysis and design at an early stage. The use of responsibility modelling as a pivotal concept appears to provide an integrating mechanism between the business process, the social system, and the technical system; the development of future alternative socio-technical scenarios using this form of representation appears to help stakeholders understand the implications of different ways of applying technology sufficiently early for them to be able to influence the direction of development.

The early experience of using these methods has been positive but has of course raised questions for subsequent research and development. One set of questions relates to the form of the socio-technical scenario that is offered to the stakeholders for evaluation. A complex set of agent relationships (as shown in Fig. 3) can be difficult to understand and daunting to interpret. It has the great advantage that it is a formal description which can be used by technical system developers to specify the demand on an information system. However, it is apparent that the more concrete we make the scenario for stakeholders, the more easily they can evaluate it. ORDIT scenarios can be dramatized so that task episodes can be enacted in role play. On occasions it has been possible to create and use videos of the scenario under investigation. There is no doubt that these are powerful ways of representing the future to help stakeholders explore the costs and benefits. It leaves open the question as to whether the act of rendering the scenario concrete causes stakeholders to respond to specific issues rather than the structural characteristics of the underlying scenario. The issue of which forms of representation will provide effective support to participative, integrated design, in which organizational, business, and technical requirements can be expressed in a valid and consistent way, forms an important topic for future research.

ACKNOWLEDGEMENTS

The ORDIT project was funded as part of the European Union ESPRIT programme (project no. 2301) and the authors wish to acknowledge the support of the European Commission and our ORDIT partners, MARI and the University of Newcastle in the UK, the Work Research Centre, Dublin, and Algotech, Rome.

REFERENCES

Andriessen, J.H.E. (1995). The why, how and what to evaluate of interaction technology: A review and proposed integration. In P. Thomas (Ed.), *CSCW requirements and evaluation* (pp. 107–124). London: Springer-Verlag.

Boehm, B., Bose, P., Horowitz, E., & Lee, M.J. (1994). Software requirements as negotiated win conditions. In *Proceedings of the international conference on Requirements Engineering* (pp. 74–83). Los Alamitos, Calif.: IEEE Computer Society Press.

Docherty, N.F., & King, M. (1995). *The consideration of organizational issues during the systems development process: An empirical analysis* (Research series paper 1995:24). Loughborough, UK: Loughborough University Business School.

Eason, K.D. (1988). *Information technology and organizational change*. London: Taylor & Francis.

Eason, K.D. (1996a). Understanding the organizational ramifications of implementing information technology systems. In E. Helander (Ed.), *Handbook of human–computer interaction*. Amsterdam, The Netherlands: North-Holland.

Eason, K.D. (1996b). Division of labour and the design of systems for computer support for co-operative work. *Journal of Information Technology, 11,* 39–50.

Eason, K.D., & Olphert, C.W. (1995). Early evaluation of the organizational implications of CSCW systems. In P. Thomas (Ed.), *CSCW requirements and evaluation* (pp. 75–89). London: Springer-Verlag.

Emery, F.E., & Trist, E.L. (1969). Socio-technical systems. In F.E. Emery (Ed.), *Systems thinking*. London: Penguin.

Hammer, M., & Champj, J. (1990). *Re-engineering the corporation: A manifesto for business revolution*. London: Nicholas Brealey.

Harker, S.D.P. (1991). Requirements specification and the role of prototyping in current practice. In J. Karat (Ed.), *Taking software design seriously: Practical techniques for human–computer interaction design*. Boston, Mass.: Academic Press.

Herbst, P.G. (1974). *Alternatives to hierarchies*. London: Tavistock.

Hornby, P., & Clegg, C. (1992). User participation in context: A case study in a UK bank. *Behaviour and Information Technology, 11*(5), 293–307.

Klein, L., & Eason, K.D. (1991). *Putting social science to work*. Cambridge, UK: Cambridge University Press.

Lyytinen, K., & Hirschheim, R. (1987). Information systems failures: A survey and classification of the empirical literature. *Oxford Surveys in Information Technology, 4*, 257–309.

Martin, M.J., & Dobson, J.E. (1991). Enterprise modelling and security policies. In S. Jajodia & C.E. Landwehr (Eds.), *Database security: Status and prospects* (Vol. IV, pp. 117–150). Amsterdam: North-Holland.

Mitroff, I.I. (1980). Management myth information systems revisited: A strategic approach to asking nasty questions about systems design. In N. Bjørn-Andersen (Ed.), *The human side of enterprise*. Amsterdam: North-Holland.

Mumford, E. (1983a). *Designing human systems*. Manchester, UK: Manchester Business School Publications.

Mumford, E. (1983b). *Designing secretaries*. Manchester, UK: Manchester Business School Publications.

Olphert, C.W., & Harker, S.D.P. (1994). The ORDIT method for organizational requirements definition. In G.E. Bradley & H.W. Hendrick (Eds.), *Human factors in organizational design and management* (Vol. 4, pp. 421–426). Amsterdam: Elsevier.

ORDIT Consortium. (1993). *ORDIT process manual*. Loughborough, UK: HUSAT Research Institute, Loughborough University of Technology.

Page, D., Williams, P., & Boyd, D. (1993). *Report of the inquiry into the London Ambulance Service*. Report commissioned by the South West Thames Regional Health Authority, 40 Eastbourne Terrace, London, W2 3QR, UK.

Preece, J. (1994). *Human–computer interaction*. Wokingham, UK: Addison-Wesley.

Rothlisberger, F.J., & Dickson, W.J. (1939). *Management and the worker*. Cambridge, Mass.: Harvard University Press.

Savage, C.M. (1990). *5th generation management: Integrating enterprises through human networking*. Bedford, Mass.: Digital Press.

Smith, A.M. (1993). *A survey of user centred design*. Unpublished MSc thesis. Loughborough, UK: Department of Computer Studies, Loughborough University of Technology.

Tapscott, D. (1982). *Office automation: A user-driven method*. New York: Plenum.

Walton, R.E. (1989). *Up and running: Integrating information technology and the organization*. Boston, Mass.: Harvard Business School.

Weisbord, M.R. (1990). *Productive workplaces: Organising and managing for dignity, meaning and community*. Oxford, UK: Jossey-Bass.

EUROPEAN JOURNAL OF WORK AND ORGANIZATIONAL PSYCHOLOGY, 1996, 5 (3), 421–438

Information System Development: From User Participation to Contingent Interaction Among Involved Parties

M.A.G. van Offenbeek

*Faculty of Management and Organization, University of Groningen,
The Netherlands*

P.L. Koopman

*Department of Work and Organizational Psychology, Vrije Universiteit
Amsterdam, The Netherlands*

Over the last few decades many social scientists have pointed to the importance of user participation in information system development (SD). In study A the opinions of 314 Dutch system developers on this issue were examined. The conclusion is that the majority rate the value of user participation highly. However, these data confront us with three important problems. First, we cannot be sure that the stated preferences of system developers are reflected in their actual behaviour. Second, system developers may give a different meaning to the concept "user participation" than social scientists. Third, "user participation" does not necessarily imply "user influence" on SD. Moreover, the empirical relationship between user participation and the effectiveness of SD remains unclear. In our opinion this can be attributed both to the multi-dimensional nature of the former concept and to the contingency of this relationship to the context of SD. Therefore, in study B, we developed a multidimensional contingency model to study the interaction among parties in SD instead of the study of user participation. In this explorative study no linear relationship between the effectiveness of SD and the interaction between users and system developers was found. Instead, effective SD seemed to require a fit between the context of SD and the interactions with and among users.

INTRODUCTION

Employee participation is a mechanism for exchanging information and creating commitment, necessary features for managerial decision making (e.g. IDE, 1981). In studies concentrating on the organizational aspects of

Requests for reprints should be addressed to Dr M.A.G. van Offenbeek, Faculty of Management and Organization, University of Groningen, postbus 800, 9700 AV Groningen, The Netherlands.

information systems development (SD), attention has been directed towards the need for "user participation" (e.g. Cressey, 1989; Hedberg, 1975; Mumford, 1983; Söderberg, 1986). "User participation" refers to the participation of employees in the development process of the system of which they will be the future users. The discussion has been concerned with the question whether, and to what extent, system developers should consult future users during the design process. The aim of user participation is to enhance both the quality of the developed system and the acceptance of this system by the future users (Ives & Olson, 1984).

A variety of research has been undertaken to determine whether user participation does indeed lead to more effective SD. Research over the last decade suggests that user participation is not a panacea for effective SD. Although Baroudi, Olson, and Ives (1986) and Riesewijk and Warmerdam (1988) have reported positive findings, Heinbokel (1994) has found a negative correlation between user involvement and overall success. Ives and Olson (1984), Algera, Koopman, and Vijlbrief (1989), and van Oostrum and Rabbie (1988) have shown that user participation has no definite effect on the effectiveness of SD. According to these studies, the conditions under which user participation will lead to better outcomes must be explained. Furthermore, the type of participation with which one is concerned should be specified. Similar conclusions have been drawn for employee participation in decision making by Heller, Drenth, Koopman, and Rus (1988). Likewise, Cotton, Vollrath, Lengnick-Hall, and Froggatt (e.g. 1990) have propagated the use of a multidimensional view on participatory leadership because its effects can vary strongly according to the form and context of the participation.

First, it can be concluded that user participation should be looked at in a more differentiated way; a one-dimensional high–low concentration of user participation has proved to be too simple. Second, the amount and kind of user participation needed depends on the context of the SD process (e.g. Edström, 1977; Schonberger, 1980; Wijnen & van Oostrum, 1993). Thus a multidimensional contingency framework for the study of the effectiveness of user participation in SD is needed.

The study of the concept "user participation" has some dysfunctional consequences from a cognitive point of view as well. We will argue that the origin of the concept makes it less suited to modern SD practices.

It is not clear what precisely is indicated by the concept of user participation. It is a semantic device which refers to many different practices. We have to specify who participates in what kind of processes and to what purpose. Do system developers participate in the change processes of user-organizations, or do users participate in the design processes of system developers? Both statements contain some truth, whereas the term "user participation" seems to refer solely to a situation in which the application of information technology is developed in isolation to its social context. The leading role is for technology, and users are brought into the design process to establish the specifications for the software. As Clegg and Symon (1989) stated "it [user participation] assumes the issue is one of getting users and others to participate with the designers who are the legitimate experts on design, and who thereby often end up owning both the problem and the solution". As such the concept leads to inferences which are inappropriate in the light of the idea that the systems built should fit the clients, in this case the prospective users.

The concept of user participation was introduced at a time when automation was characterized by a technological push and the term bears testimony to this. Nowadays we find a much stronger demand pull: the automation market is shrinking and organizations have far more knowledge about information technology than in earlier days. Nevertheless, case studies of SD have shown that technicians too often still dominate the SD process (Björn-Andersen, Eason, & Robey, 1986; Child & Loveridge, 1990; Heming, 1992; Riesewijk & Warmerdam, 1988).

When system developers are told that they should allow for user participation, this in a way reinforces the domination of SD by automation experts. In fact, the concept of "users" only exists in the minds of automation experts. In their own eyes the former are workers (either operational, professional, or managerial) making use of an automated system in the accomplishment of their tasks. This reminds us of the fact that system developers are regularly heard complaining that users have no knowledge of their own needs. According to Mumford (1983), this problem frequently has to do with the abstractness of the context in which system developers try to elicit their clients needs. We would like to add that their own roles are often unclear to the users. Users may be committed in a passive way, but they do not directly see how they can claim an active role. Both the inadequate knowledge of the users and the indefinite nature of their roles stem from the fact that the orientation is all too often a technically determined one, whereas we can conceive of many SD scenarios in which the imperative does not lie with the technicians (e.g. Frese, Prümper, & Solzbacher, 1994; Robinson & Hayes, 1994).

Given the central role of system developers in SD, what is their own opinion of user participation? This question was treated in study A, which is reported in the next section. The results show that to a large extent system developers have embraced the concept of user participation. The majority are of the opinion that user participation is needed for effective SD. However, these findings confront us with three important problems. First, because of the technical imperative that was discussed in the last paragraph, user participation does not necessarily imply user influence on SD. Second, we cannot be sure that the stated preferences of system developers are reflected in their actual behaviour. Third, system developers may give a different meaning to the concept of user participation than social scientists.

Hence, we also needed study B in which the effectiveness of the interaction among parties in SD processes was studied. Studying the interactions among groups in SD has some advantages over studying user participation. First, because by doing this the technical orientation to which the term "user participation" bears testimony is replaced by a managerial orientation. Second, because it stresses the two-sided nature of the exchanges between system developers and their clients. The influence of future users can only be realized by interaction (whether written or oral, direct, or indirect), which is inevitably a two-sided phenomenon. The participation of a group in an SD process can have no direct effect on the outcomes of SD: It is the interaction among and within the groups involved that determines the outcomes. In this respect it is interesting to note that Brodbeck (1994) has reported that the negative correlation between user participation and project effectiveness was greatly diminished by communication density in the project. As Weick (1979) has pointed out, human interaction is crucial in situations where organizational members are faced with equivocality. While user participation may be common practice (Wijnen & van Oostrum, 1993), the involvement can still be largely symbolic (Baroudi et al., 1986).

A third reason is that we should look at users in a more differentiated way. "The users" as a homogeneous group of people does not exist and if it ever did, certainly does so no longer. Nowadays, the control of SD processes requires far more differentiated questions than whether or not users should participate.

Now we come to our fourth and final argument. As in decision making (Heller et al., 1988), the rationale for participation in system development has cognitive as well as political components: information is exchanged and power is exerted. User participation refers to the interaction between designer and user. The people who will work with the new system do not only have interests as users but also as employees (Doorewaard, 1985). As users they want systems that are (amongst other things) reliable and usable. As employees they are interested in subjects such as work security, payment, stress, and autonomy. If future users work together with system developers during the design phase, this interaction may not lead to the fulfilment of their interests as employees. Promotion of these interests calls for interaction between management and operational workers, and probably also between different intra- or inter-organizational groups. The concept of user participation diverts the attention from the political component of the interaction processes by sustaining a unitary orientation towards SD (Blacker & Brown, 1986), an orientation which does not fit practices that are potentially pluralist in nature and will be even more so in the future (for instance groupware, electronic data interchange, integration of information systems, business network re-engineering).

The organizational and cognitive psychological arguments that have been discussed thus far lead to the conclusion that an interaction model is needed that allows for:

- describing interaction in SD in a multidimensional way
- specifying the meaning of critical contextual factors
- adopting a managerial instead of a technical orientation
- stressing the two-sided nature of interaction
- making a distinction between different user and other groups involved
- displaying a pluralist orientation to SD as opposed to a unitary orientation
- discerning cognitive as well as political functions of interaction.

In study B, we will report the development of such a multidimensional contingency model in which both the interaction among the groups involved in SD and the context of the SD process can be described. The context is defined to consist of five types of risk to effective SD. Different risk profiles will call for different interactions among the groups involved in SD. We will describe some of the results of our explorative in-depth study of seven cases.

STUDY A: A SYSTEM DEVELOPERS AND "USER PARTICIPATION"

We administered a survey on the topic of organizing the information system development process. One of the aims of this study was to determine whether system developers favour a user-oriented working style, that is, to what extent do they prefer the participation of users. In this section we will present the data concerning the opinions of system developers about user participation in SD.

Method and Subjects

In order to determine whether system developers favour a user-oriented working style, we asked respondents to rate their personally favoured style of working on four five-point scale items with opposite poles: "Which working style do you yourself enjoy the most?" We wanted to know whether the differences in user orientedness are related to the type of employment (e.g. user organization, software firm) and type of automation (technical versus administrative). As can be seen in Table 1, other independent variables were the level and type of education, and years of experience.

The extent to which system developers enjoy a user-oriented working style does not tell us whether they perceive a positive relationship between user participation and the effectiveness of SD. Do system developers believe that user participation is needed for effective SD? We asked the respondents

TABLE 1
Variables in Study A

Dependent Variables	Independent Variables
User orientedness	Type of employment
Perceived ideal SD approach	Type of automation
Perceived critical causes of success	Level and type of education
Perceived critical causes of failure	Years of experience

whether they think that an ideal approach exists for system development. If the answer was "yes" we invited them to name the five most important elements of this approach. This question was open-ended, but the respondent could pick items from an enclosed list of 50 approach characteristics drawn from the SD literature. One of the listed characteristics was "active user participation". Furthermore, respondents were asked to report the perceived causes of the outcome of two automation processes in which they had participated; one successful, the other not. This question was also open-ended.

The addresses of 600 system developers with two or more years of experience were drawn in a random way from the database of a free journal widely read among automation practitioners. The usable response rate was 52% ($N = 314$). According to our comparison of the background variables of the database population and the respondents, we have no reason to believe that the non-response was selective. The fact that only a few of the questions concerned user participation reduces the possibility that subjects with a negative attitude to user participation did not respond.

Results of Study A

Almost 100% of the respondents see "good usability for the end users" as a critical criterion for the success of SD. An indicator "user-orientedness" was derived by summing the scores on the four items in Table 2 and dividing them by four. A high user-orientedness (score >3) was found for 226 respondents (72%). Table 2 shows that the majority (89%) personally prefer to make use of "active user participation", indicating that user participation is not often seen as a handicap by Dutch system developers. We did find that respondents in technical automation are less user-oriented than those who developed only administrative information systems (regression analysis, $P < 0.05$, 6% explained variance). A possible explanation may be found in the fact that subjects in technical automation reported cases with an average of 10 workstations, while subjects in administrative automation reported on average cases with more than 100 workstations. Because the former have to deal with fewer users, a user-oriented working style may be easier to

TABLE 2
Personally Favoured Working Style, Distribution of Percentages Per Item (N = 314)

Personal Preference for . . .*	Score 1, 2 (%)	Neutral 3 (%)	Score 4, 5 (%)	Personal Preference for . . .*
Minimal user participation	3	9	**89**	Active user participation
Few participating users	30	26	**44**	Many participating users
Automation expert as project leader	**43**	19	38	User as project leader
The role of an expert who devises the design and/or other products	26	15	**59**	The role of a supporter with expertise

*Five point scale: 1, 2 = preference left-side alternative; 4, 5 = preference right-side alternative; 3 = neutral.

realize in technical automation. However, it does not say anything about the intensity of user participation needed in technical automation. On the whole the independent variables (Table 1) explained less than 10% of the variance in preference for a user-oriented working style.

Two hundred and nine respondents think that an ideal approach for SD does exist. In Table 3 the most frequently mentioned characteristics of their "ideal approach" are listed. "Active user participation" is top of the list; 43% mention it as an essential element.

In 26% of the reported successful automation processes (N = 283) user participation was declared to have been a critical success factor. In 20.6% of the processes that were not successful, a shortage of user participation was attributed to be a critical cause of failure (N = 265). In only two of the processes reported was "too much user participation" attributed to be a cause of failure. More generally, the respondents referred to communication, including user participation, as a critical factor in 47% of the successful cases and in 28% of the failed cases.

TABLE 3
The Most Frequently Mentioned Characteristics of "The Ideal Approach" (N = 209)

Characteristic	% of Respondents
Active user participation	42.5
Realistic planning and alert monitoring	38.2
A good atmosphere in the team	23.7
Explicit definition of aims and expectancies	22.7
A multidisciplinary team	20.3

Discussion

From these data it can be concluded that the majority of Dutch system developers prefer a user-oriented working style. Moreover, many system developers think that user participation is needed for effective SD. This result is in accordance with Cressey and Williams (1991), who have reported that the user participation that did actually take place is by and large evaluated positively. Nevertheless, our study has some limitations.

The question remains whether the stated preference of the system developers is in accordance with their behaviour. Heinbokel (1994) has found that high user-orientedness does not necessarily lead to more interaction with users.

Further, system developers may have something different in mind when they speak about user participation than social scientists. The results of Gould and Lewis (1987) suggest that system developers in the United States identify, stereotype, or describe who the users are, rather than trying to understand them. They hear the users and read what others wrote about them instead of getting into direct contact with the users. The system developers present their design to the users and let them sign off on their design instead of interacting prior to the design phase.

Finally, user participation does not necessarily enable employees to have a substantive influence on the systems with which they will perform their tasks. This will depend on the interaction realized during SD. In a European survey, Cressey and Williams (1991) interviewed 7326 persons about user participation. They found that user participation became substantial rather late in the process, when many decisions had already been made and the room for influence had become limited (see also Vijlbrief, Algera, & Koopman, 1986).

The acknowledgement of system developers that user participation is needed is important, but as in the three problems mentioned previously show, this finding results in an array of questions: Which categories of potential users interact with whom, when, how, and to what purpose in effective SD, and which contextual factors influence these relationships?

STUDY B: FROM USER PARTICIPATION TO CONTINGENT INTERACTION

Method and Cases

In this study we have explored how a match could be realized between contextual characteristics and SD approach, in order to develop a successful information system. Existing theory was used to develop a contingency framework, composed of three main variables: context, approach, and outcome (van Offenbeek, 1993). Within this contingency framework, propositions about the matching of context and approach were formulated and tested preliminarily (van Offenbeek & Koopman, in press). One aspect of an SD approach is the choice of which interaction should take place among the groups involved. Within the scope of this article we will not draw upon the other aspects of an SD approach—see van Offenbeek and Koopman (1996).

The case material consists of the retrospective analyses of seven processes in which a data processing and/or operational and/or tactical management information system was developed. The cases were selected on the basis of two criteria: (1) the SD process should involve at least some social and/or organizational issues, and (2) variance among the cases in context variables. Because we were confronted with substantive changes in the context and/or approach variables in some cases, we subdivided those cases into different episodes to be analysed separately. This resulted in 10 episodes, of which five could be considered to be failures and five to be successes (Table 4).

Data collection took place during the last phases of SD and consisted of semi-structured interviews with key actors (developers, users, management) and by the analysis of documents. Six months after the implementation of the system, questionnaires were filled out by users and managers. The data from the interviews and the documents were used to determine the characteristics of context and approach. Three judges rated the cases according to the context variables. The mean interjudge agreement, corrected for coincidence, was satisfactory: 0.87. The questionnaires were used to evaluate the outcome of the SD process. The indicator for the success of SD was whether the resulting information system was actually implemented and used on a regular basis—a dichotomous measure.

TABLE 4
Total Scores for Risks and Measures Taken in 10 Episodes of SD

Case	Total Score Risks (max. 8)	Total Score Approach Measures (max. 40)
Successes		
A2	0	12
B2	1	21
C2	2	27
D2	6	30
E	6	35
Failures		
B1 (system rejected)	1	5–9
C1 (project cancelled)	6	16
D1 (major stagnation)	7	18
F	3	16
G	4	16

Because the scope of the article is confined to the interaction with and among users groups in SD, we will limit ourselves to the introduction of the context and interaction variables.

An Interaction Model in SD Processes

We will describe two components of the contingency framework: the interaction model and the context variables (see Fig. 1). Ashmos, McDaniel, and Duchon (1990) formulated a model to describe the type of participation in decison making. We adapted this model in order to make it suitable for the description of the interaction within SD. The number of context factors is almost infinite. We limited ourselves to those context factors that cause a risk in terms of the effectiveness of the SD process. According to contingency theory, these risks can be controlled by choosing a fitting approach. This means that the interactions, as one of the aspects of SD approach, should match the risks in a specific SD process. We distinguished five risk types that can be used to specify the context of the information system development process.

Attributes of the Interaction Model

First it should be established who could potentially be involved in SD. The *number of people* having to interact together can vary strongly depending on the context and the function of the interaction. For some

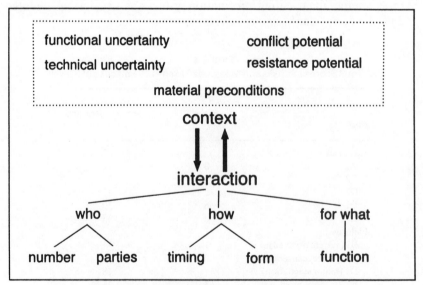

FIG. 1.   Context factors and interaction model in SD.

activities in SD more participants will lead to a better result: the greater the number of direct users learning to handle the system, the more effective the implementation. For other activities there will be an optimum: when future users have to test the programs constructed, one user will not be sufficient to track down all the bugs and inconveniences. For most of the time, however, it would be highly inefficient if 50 future users were to test the system. Still, for some activities more interaction will be less effective: one person should be responsible for the conceptual integrity of the system.

The next attribute is formed by the *parties* who have to interact. This attribute also varies according to the context and the development activity involved. Parties that may be involved in SD are the board of directors, middle line management, automation experts, personnel managers, trade union representatives, and, of course, the (operational and managerial) workers who will use the system. The relevant groups should be assessed locally. Users should not be treated as a homogenous group. They will often have to be split into functional, geographical, vertical and/or horizontal categories. The same goes for the technicians: "why, with whom, and how" will be answered differently for a database specialist, a programmer, an information analyst, or an information systems manager.

We are not only concerned with the question of who has to interact with whom but also with the attributes describing how interactions are to be realized. The *timing of the interaction* determines in which phase(s) the interaction takes place. We have chosen a global life cycle model specifying the most important activities: initiation, analysis, design, realization, implementation, and use and maintenance. Sometimes implementation will be the starting point of a subsequent life cycle (incremental change). Moreover, in processes with many iterations among activities the distinctions between successive stages within one life cycle will be vague.

Many different *forms* of interaction can be found in SD. The form is defined by the extent to which the interaction is either formal or informal (Ashmos et al., 1990), direct or indirect (Blackler & Brown, 1986), and by its intensity (Vroom & Jago, 1988). The form of interaction can be very important. For instance, as formal task descriptions often do not describe tasks accurately, local observation and analysis of the actual task activities has been suggested (e.g. Frese, 1987; Rogard, 1990).

The last, but by no means the least, important attribute is the *function of interaction*. Ives and Olson (1984) mention two global aims of user participation: to realize increased system quality and to heighten user acceptance of the system. We have extended these into four functions of interaction, the first two cognitive, the last two political: factual exchange, learning, motivating, and negotiating.

The realization of high system quality calls for interaction directed towards the *factual exchange* of information. For example, exchanges between users and automation experts in order to establish the specifications, between programmers working on different subsystems to establish interface specifications, or between management and workers about the planned change. Most of the time *learning processes* are also needed to achieve this aim. They lead to a better insight for the parties into the specific system and a better understanding of information systems in general. Learning processes may be needed in order to reach a better understanding of (1) goals, problems, and the functioning of their own organization, (2) the meaning of the changes proposed, (3) the functions automation can and cannot fulfil, and (4) the consequences automation will have for the organization.

The second of Ives and Olson's aims concerns the *motivational function* of interaction. Interaction is critical in establishing a high level of acceptance. Organizational members should feel themselves to be the owners of the system and all parties should feel committed to the system's goals and concept. Usually, conflicting points of view, interests and incompatible needs and practices will occur. They can lead to conflicts about the development that have to be recognized and tackled. This brings us to the fourth function of interaction: Interaction can also facilitate processes of *negotiation and power*.

Of course this classification is an analytical one. Empirically the distinction between the functions can be blurred. Sometimes interaction will be directed towards different functions at the same time, sometimes the functions will concern interaction activities that are clearly separated in time and place.

The Context of SD: Five Risk Types

Once in a while SD processes will occur that are relatively simple and to which principles of linearity, objectivity, and technical rationality can be successfully applied. In these circumstances, the dominant actors can choose the most efficient approach, because the dominant actors do not have to take measures for risks that are low. That is what we have called the "efficiency proposition". However, perhaps more often than not, organizational reality is not simple and ordered in a known way, but complex, ambiguous, and unstable. Moreover, not everyone has the same objectives, interests, and views. In addition, system developers can be confronted by time and money constraints. Thus, risks can be cognitive, political, or material in nature. The following five risk types were distinguished: functional and technical uncertainty (cognitive), conflict potential and resistance potential (political), and material preconditions.

Functional Uncertainty   refers to the risk that the actors will choose the wrong solution or solve the wrong problem. The magnitude of this risk is determined by the characteristics of the task system in the existing situation and of the (expected) changes to the task system. A high complexity, a low stability of the tasks, and having no acquaintance with the tasks to which the system development is directed, will heighten the functional uncertainty with which the system developers are confronted, as will obscurity of the problem(s), unknown goal(s) or needs, and the absence of criteria by which the solution will be judged. Two other potential factors are the anticipated extensiveness of the changes in the task system, and a lack of experience with SD on the part of the organizational members.

Technical Uncertainty refers to the risk that the conceptualized solution cannot be realized. The magnitude of this risk is determined by the characteristics of the technological aspect system in the existing situation, and by the technological aspects of the change. In system development this risk increases when the existing technological system is complex and relatively new; when technical experts are unacquainted with the software environment, the complexity of the system realization is high, and the quality and commitment of the technical experts is low.

Conflict Potential refers to the risk that incompatible needs and interests will hamper problem solving. It is determined by the degree of pluralism in the existing structure as compared with its desired uniformity. This type of risk is increased when more parties whose ideas, language, and/or interests are heterogenous are involved and when the scope of the SD process (in terms of people and finance) is large. This risk is also increased when the required integration among the parties is high and when the development is dependent on third parties or on the results or progress of other projects.

Resistance Potential refers to the risk that members of the organization will be dissatisfied with the realized solution, because they feel its implementation would decrease the quality of their working life. The magnitude of this risk is determined by the changeability of the organizational members concerned, compared with characteristics of the wanted change. The risk is increased when the workers (management) have a low change potential, a low willingness to change, and when the qualitative and quantitative impact on the work organization is high.

Material Preconditions refer to the risk that the SD process will not pay for itself or will be aborted prematurely due to lack of resources. This risk is defined as the amount of energy needed, as compared with the amount available, i.e. budget, in terms of human, machine, and computer resources, time pressure, and the importance of the SD process. Material preconditions define the extent to which an approach needs to be efficient.

Results of Study B

In this section we will first give a brief summary of the most important results of the study. More detailed results about the contingency framework as a whole and the individual cases can be found in van Offenbeek and Koopman (in press). Next, we will concentrate on the way in which a fit between context and interaction was realized. These results are tentative, as the study was explorative and consisted of only 10 episodes.

The analysis examined whether one or a combination of risk types, or one or a combination of approach characteristics, could explain the outcome of the 10 SD processes (Table 4). This was not possible. However, the match between the risk factors and the approach characteristics was able to explain the success or the failure of each case. Thus, we found some support for the efficiency proposition: In the case of one or more low risks, an efficient approach, that is an approach without measures to control these risks, led to success. When faced with high risks, a positive outcome was only found when measures to control them had been taken. Our findings suggest that when moderate risks are perceived, control measures should also be taken.

Interaction in the Case of High Functional Uncertainty.   When functional uncertainty is high, users will have to interact at an early stage with the automation experts, because early in the process the capacity to process information will be highest (Davis & Olson, 1985); people are more open minded as many decisions have not yet been taken. The interaction must be directed towards the exchange of information and learning. However, when the resistance potential is also high (see later), and no room is created for negotiations, the interaction between users and developers during SD will turn into "mock participation". In this case interaction between users and system developers will be counterproductive (Algera et al., 1989; Markus, 1983; Söderberg, 1986).

Interaction in the Case of High Technical Uncertainty.   This risk requires interactions among the system developers. Exchange of information and collective learning will be the most important functions of the interaction. As in the case of high functional uncertainty, the exchange of information alone will not be sufficient to control high technical uncertainty. Learning will have to occur because the participants have little experience with the technology and methods and/or have to improve their skills. Proven technology and/or methods are not available. Because of the learning function, we found that interaction cannot be confined to written communication and formal meetings. Both formal and informal interaction is necessary. Line management and SD management should interact to inform each other of

the feasibility of the proposed solution as well as of the available alternatives.

Interaction in the Case of High Conflict Potential.   When heterogenous
groups are involved it is more difficult to create shared meaning and consensus because group members will be less prone to behaviour favouring
and supporting other groups (Algera et al., 1989; Vroom & Jago, 1988).
The values and norms will be questioned. Therefore, in cases with a high
conflict potential, prior to interacting with system developers about specifications, representatives of the organizational groups involved should
interact with one another. Representational forms of interaction will prohibit a Tower of Babel-like chaos. Formal co-ordination of the interactions
is necessary to unequivocally take and record decisions and communicate
them to the grassroots and others involved. This early interaction should be
directed towards collective learning and negotiation. In this way ideas and
experiences can be exchanged, differences in points of view and interests
can be explicated, and the goals of the SD process can be negotiated. Negotiation will be the most important function of the interaction. It will be the
responsibility of the dominant actors to manage the process towards shared
meaning. Bouwen and Fry (1991), indeed, found a learning-confrontation
strategy to be more successful in these circumstances.

Interaction in the Case of High Resistance Potential.   The responsible
line managers will have to interact with all the workers to generate the
commitment needed (Vroom & Jago, 1988). The most important function
of this interaction is enhancing motivation. Moreover, resistance has a cognitive base as uncertainty heightens resistance. Therefore, a sufficient
exchange of information between the dominant actors and all those involved
is necessary. Everyone should know what is going to happen when, and
what consequences this will have on the quality of his or her work. Furthermore, in order to ensure that workers will be able to function effectively in
a changing or new work environment, individual learning, e.g. courses, is
necessary. A short time-lag between learning activities and implementation
prevents people forgetting their new knowledge and skills and returning to
old habits and methods.

Material Preconditions   define the extent to which the SD process has
to be efficient. If resources are limited, one is forced to be economical with
the number of people that engage in interactions. When the preconditions
are insufficient to realize the necessary interaction activities, the process
should be redefined in order to make the SD context less risky. This could
be accomplished by limiting the target groups or the functional purposes of
the system.

CONCLUSIONS

The majority of (Dutch) system developers rate the value of user participation highly (study A). However, we have argued that additional questions about the issue of user participation would benefit from research into the interaction processes within SD, and that these interaction processes should match the risk factors of a specific SD process (study B). To sum up, by using the interaction model presented, some advantages are to be gained.

- Interaction can be specified between different groups at different phases for different reasons and in different ways.
- Alternative possibilities for interaction with and among users can be explicated.
- Responsibilities for interaction can be located in time and towards function.
- The interaction model offers a broader concept than that of user participation, fitting the pluralist nature of current development practices better.
- The model stresses the dual nature of interaction.

We believe that this model, together with the risk types, enables the formulation and testing of contingency hypotheses concerning the interaction needed for effective SD. In our study we have only made a start (van Offenbeek & Koopman, in press). The practical purpose of such research will be to offer practitioners more accurate contingency guidelines concerning the interaction with and among groups involved in SD. Nevertheless, the effectiveness of SD is not only dependent on the right kinds of interaction, but also on other aspects of the SD approach, notably the definition and orientation of, and the differentiation and co-ordination within, the SD process (van Offenbeek & Koopman, 1996). The interaction in SD should also be congruent with these other aspects of the approach.

ACKNOWLEDGEMENT

We would like to thank Prof. Dr M. Frese for his comments on an earlier version of this article.

REFERENCES

Algera, J.A., Koopman, P.L., & Vijlbrief, H.P.J. (1989). Management strategies in introducing computer-based information systems. *Applied Psychology: An International Review, 38*, 1.

Ashmos, D.P., McDaniel Jr., R.R., & Duchon, D. (1990). Differences in perception of strategic decision-making processes: The case of physicians and administrators. *Journal of Applied Behavioral Science, 26*(2), 201–218.

Baroudi, J.J., Olson, M.H., & Ives, B. (1986). An empirical study of the impact of user involvement on system usage and information satisfaction. *Communications of the Association for Computing Machinery, 29*(3), 232–238.

Björn-Andersen, N., Eason, K., & Robey, D. (1986). *Managing computer impact: An international study of management and organisation.* Norwood, NJ: Ablex Publishing.

Blackler, F.H.M., & Brown, C. (1986). Alternative models to guide the design and introduction of new information technologies into work organisations. *Journal of Occupational Psychology, 59*, 287–313.

Bouwen, R., & Fry, R. (1991). Organisational innovation and learning: Four patterns of dialogue between the dominant logic and the new logic. *International Studies in Management and Organisation, 21*(4), 37–51.

Brodbeck, F.C. (1994, July). *Empirical results about communication and performance in software development projects.* Paper presented at the 23rd international congress of Applied Psychology, Madrid, Spain.

Child, J., & Loveridge, R. (1990). *Information technology in European services: Towards a micro-electronic future.* Oxford, UK: Basil Blackwell.

Clegg, C., & Symon, G. (1989). *A review of human-centred manufacturing technology and a framework for its design and evaluation* (Sheffield Memo. No. 1036). University of Sheffield.

Cotton, J.L., Vollrath, D.A., Lengnick-Hall, M.L., & Froggatt, K.L. (1990). In fact the form of participation does matter—A rebuttal to Leana, Locke and Schweiger. *Academy of Management Review, 15*(1), 147–153.

Cressey, P. (1989). *Trends in employee participation and new technology.* Glasgow, UK: University of Glasgow.

Cressey, P., & Williams, R. (1991). *Inspraak in verandering; nieuwe technologie en de rol van inspraak van werknemers* (Report No. SY-58-90-384-NL-C). Luxemburg: Bureau voor officiële publikaties der europese gemeenschappen.

Davis, G.B., & Olson, M.H. (1985). *Management information systems.* New York: McGraw-Hill.

Doorewaard, J.A.C.M. (1985). Kantoren in actie. In *Technologie en arbeid in de jaren tachtig en negentig.* Nederland: FNV/cmhp.

Edström, A. (1977). User influence and the success of MIS-projects: A contingency approach. *Human Relations, 30*, 589–607.

Frese, M. (1987). Human–computer interaction in the office. In C.L. Cooper & I.T. Robertson (Eds.), *International review of industrial and organisational psychology.* Chichester, UK: Wiley & Sons Ltd.

Frese, M., Prümper, J., & Solzbacher, F. (1994). Eine Fallstudie zu Benutzerbeteiligung und Prototyping. In F.C. Brodbeck & M. Frese (Eds.), *Produktivität und Qualität in Software-Projekten.* Munich, Germany: Oldenbourg.

Gould, J.D., & Lewis, C. (1987). Designing for usability key principles and what designers think. In R.M. Baecker & W.A.S. Buxton (Eds.), *Readings in human–computer interaction: A multidisciplinary approach.* San Mateo, Calif.: Morgan Kaufmann.

Hedberg, B. (1975). Computer systems to support industrial democracy. In E. Mumford & H. Sackman (Eds.), *Human choice and computers.* Amsterdam: North Holland.

Heinbokel, T. (1994). Benutzerbeteiligung Schlüssel zum Erfolg oder Hemmschuh der Entwicklung? In F.C. Brodbeck & M. Frese (Eds.), *Produktivität und Qualität in Software-Projekten.* Munich, Germany: Oldenbourg.

Heller, F.A., Drenth, P.J.D., Koopman, P.L., & Rus, V. (1988). *Decisions in organisations: A three country comparative study.* London: Sage.

Heming, B.H.J. (1992). *Kwaliteit van arbeid, geautomatiseerd.* Unpublished doctoral dissertation. Faculteit der Wijsbegeerte en Technische Maatschappijwetenschappen, Delft, The Netherlands.

IDE. (1981). *Industrial democracy in Europe*. Oxford, UK: Clarendon Press.

Ives, B., & Olson, M.H. (1984). User involvement and MIS success. A review of research. *Management Science, 30*, 586–603.

Markus, M.L. (1983). Power, politics and MIS implementation. *Communications of the Association for Computing Machinery, 26*, 430–444.

Mumford, E. (1983). *Designing human systems for new technology: The ETHICS method*. Manchester, UK: Manchester Business School.

Offenbeek, M.A.G. van. (1993). *Van methode naar scenarios*. PhD thesis, Free University, Amsterdam.

Offenbeek, M.A.G. van, & Koopman, P.L. (1996). Interaction and decision-making in project teams. In M.A. West (Ed.), *Handbook of work group psychology*. Chichester, UK: Wiley.

Offenbeek, M.A.G. van, & Koopman, P.L. (in press). Scenarios for system development: Matching context and approach. *Behavior and Information Technology*.

Oostrum, J. van, & Rabbie, J.M. (1988). Inspraak en effectiviteit; een contingentiebenadering. *Gedrag en Organisatie, 1*(2), 55–70.

Riesewijk, B., & Warmerdam, J. (1988). *Het slagen en falen van automatiseringsprojecten*. Nijmegen, The Netherlands: Nijmegen instituut voor toegepast sociaal wetenschappelijk onderzoek.

Rogard, V. (1990, September). *How and why to improve the computer design methods by work analysis*. Paper presented at the workshop on Technological change process and its impact on work, Siofok, Hungary.

Schonberger, R.J. (1980). MIS design: A contingency approach. *MIS Quarterly, March*, 13–20.

Söderberg, I. (1986, May). *Office work and office automation—user participation under change*. Paper presented at the international scientific conference on Work with Display Units, Stockholm, Sweden.

Vijlbrief, H.P.J., Algera, J.A., & Koopman, P.L. (1986). *Management of automation projects*. Paper presented at the 2nd West European conference on the Psychology of Work and Organisation, Aachen, Germany.

Vroom, V.H., & Jago, A.G. (1988). *The new leadership managing participation in organisations*. Englewood Cliffs, NJ: Prentice-Hall.

Weick, K.E. (1979). *The social psychology of organizing*. Philippines: Addison-Wesley.

Wijnen, B.J., & Oostrum, J. van (1993). Een contingentiemodel voor de invoering van geautomatiseerde informatiesystemen. *Mans en Onderwering, 2*, 88–103.

EUROPEAN JOURNAL OF WORK AND ORGANIZATIONAL PSYCHOLOGY, 1996, 5 (3), 439–456

Modelling Group Decision Making: Some Important Aspects for System Design

Edeltraud Hanappi-Egger

Department for Computer Supported Co-operative Work,
Technical University of Vienna, Vienna, Austria

The discussion on work flexibility in organizations seems to be promising in terms of self-determination and autonomy of the concerned people. Computer systems offer features to articulate preferences of tasks and times. Therefore the work planning process could be more democratic, since the workers could participate in the decision-making procedure actively. The article investigates how a decision situation can be modelled in order to design a technical support system. In addition it will be analysed as to which social and group dynamic aspects play crucial roles—from a system designer's view. Empirical data on time management processes of various working groups serves as discussion example.

INTRODUCTION

Since decisions are based on information, the fundamental idea emerged that "the better the information, the better the decision". In consequence, ways of offering as much information as possible were looked for and the support of computer systems for decision makers was developed further. In the meantime many technical systems—subsumed as "decision support systems"—are available. A new application field for those decision support systems (DSSs) seems to be Computer Supported Co-operative Work (CSCW).

Grudin (1994) states that CSCW is nothing more than a synonym for GDSS—Group Decision Support Systems. Nevertheless CSCW seems to be a special type of GDSS: Assuming that, as the notion of Computer Supported Co-operative Work suggests, a group of people has to accomplish a common task, the decision and therefore the bargaining process is limited to task–time–person assignments (Egger & Hanappi, 1994b). Contrary to pure process-automation, where working people are treated as resources being assigned to certain tasks, CSCW pre-supposes that group members

---

Requests for reprints should be addressed to E. Hanappi-Egger, Department for CSCW, Technical University of Vienna, Argentinierstr. 8/187, A-1040 Vienna, Austria.

are in a position to formulate personal preferences and, at least partially, can realize them. This is exactly what defines the scope of negotiations. In other words, the decision to be made can be described as the result of a bargaining situation concerning the distribution of tasks among members of a working group. In order to support groups by providing them with a technical system, a basic framework has to be designed, which is a representation of the group's setting. Implementing a group decision support system therefore means to build a model of the decision-making situation. Since bargaining over work distribution has a rather strong social dimension and requires the consideration of many different planning parameters, its support by technical features seems to be justified. As a consequence rather complex models have to be developed representing these social processes adequately. From a system design's point of view it is obvious that modelling bargaining in social groups requires sophisticated description tools, a statement which will be discussed in more detail later.

Therefore, the theme of this article, namely modelling bargaining situations, leads to the necessity to consider existing decision theories and to assess them in respect of their applicability to working groups. Since the article will concentrate on decision making in work processes, several case-studies of time management are presented. The empirical investigations will not be presented in detail, since they shall serve for discussion only. The main idea is to highlight the problems a system designer has to face when modelling bargaining situations. Therefore the case-studies are used to illustrate various social and group-dynamic aspects indicating the limits of automatization.

DECISION THEORIES

The framework of decision theory is based on the concept of probability: Indeed it would be easy to choose out of a finite set of possible actions with sure outcome, since the outcomes can be directly compared and the optimal one can be determined. All that is needed would be a consistent preference order of the decision maker. What has to be considered as "consistent" has been the topic of a whole branch of microeconomics, namely utility theory (Kreps, 1990). The results of this research are that today a common view on the notion of so-called "well-behaved" utility functions exists which vice versa is used to define the rationality of decison makers. Taking into account that real live processes can hardly be described in the mentioned way, but are always characterized by risk, uncertainty, and even incomplete information, leads to the necessary inclusion of random processes and expectation formation. As a consequence the easiest possible extension is to combine the utility of each outcome with its expected probability. This single number between 0 and 1 is thought to incorporate all random elements related to the respective outcome. An interesting question is where these probabilities come from. Keynes (1921) held that there is a strong subjective component in the generation of probabilities used by decision makers. In other words, personal experiences and attitudes play a crucial role in the assessment of outcomes' probabilities. This is somehow in contradiction to the mainstream view, where the distribution of observed realizations is the starting point for the notion of probability. As far as several independent decision makers might observe past realizations, directly or indirectly, these probabilities assume a more "objective" character. In a sense the opposition between these views has been bridged by Bayes (1764), whose concept of learning expresses their mutual dependence: Subjective probabilities are learned from objective realizations, while it is rather subjective what is to be considered as objective realization. In any case it seems to be not trivial to derive probabilities of future events. Therefore in decision-theory literature a further distinction concerning the knowledge of the decision maker is widely used (compare Arrow, 1971): If the probability of an event is known and less than 1 (in other words "certainty" is excluded), then the respective decision is called "risky"; if only the type of the distribution function of the event is given, then the respective decision is called "uncertain" while if even this information is missing the respective decision is made under "incomplete information". Learning could lead from incomplete information via uncertainty to risky decision making (see also Hirshleifer & Riley, 1992).

Once the probability is given, the decision process can be presented as follows (for the first treatment of the axioms necessary to guarantee the existence of these probabilities see Ramsey, 1931). (See Fig. 1.)

The decision situation is characterized by a single decision maker with a utility function and a set of possible actions (see also Rapoport, 1980). Each action with a certain probability leads to a certain outcome. If outcomes are evaluated by the use of the utility function and are weighed by their respective probabilities, then the decision maker arrives at a set of expected utilities. Finally the action with the highest expected utility will be chosen. Some authors (e.g. Rhodes, 1993) call the first phase of this decision-making process "decision" and the second phase "choice": While "decision" includes the steps till the calculation of expected utilities, "choice" refers to the search for an optimum of the latter. Note that the approach of decision theory assumes that a decision maker is confronted with a certain "state of the world" (Gravelle & Rees, 1981) with random elements. This view turns out to be a quite adequate tool to describe situations in which the possible actions are not mutually dependent on actions of other decision makers. Such decision-making processes could concern expected consumption with a large number of single consumers: Instead of costly consideration of the involved parties an average probability of their behaviour is taken. In many other situations where random natural events such as future weather are

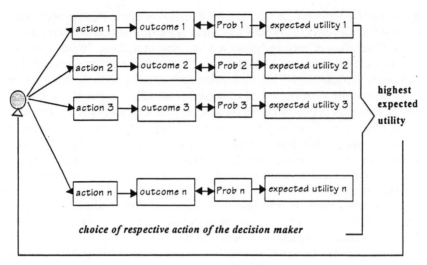

FIG. 1.   Decision-making process based on decision theory.

important, there is no other way than taking expected probabilities. There is, of course, permanent criticism of the mainstream paradigm, both on a theoretical level (e.g. Shackle, 1949) and on empirical grounds (e.g. Allais, 1953).

Nevertheless a great deal of decision-making situations appear to be characterized by a mutual dependency between several decision makers. In other words, decisions of a single decision maker influence the expected payoffs and therefore the decisions of other decision makers, who vice versa will consider the already-made decisions for their own decisions. Decision theory of course could deal with these situations, too—but not in a sophisticated way. Summarizing, the strategic behaviour of an opponent in a single figure such as a probability, while it actually could be anticipated in more detail, clearly neglects available information. This is exactly the starting point of game theory considerations.

Since game theory deals with interpersonal decision-making processes, it can be understood as an extension of decision theory. Instead of summarizing the influence of other decision makers in single probabilities of the respective influenced outcomes, the whole decision processes of the others, including their prospective outcomes, are taken into the picture. Figure 2 depicts the new situation.

In Fig. 2 only the interdependence between two decision makers with two possible actions is shown. Evidently the model of the opponent replaces probabilities. Now the assumptions about strategic behaviour of the other, captured in this model, are the source of uncertainty.

A major advantage of the game theory formulation is that the source of uncertainty can be made more explicit by stating what a decision maker

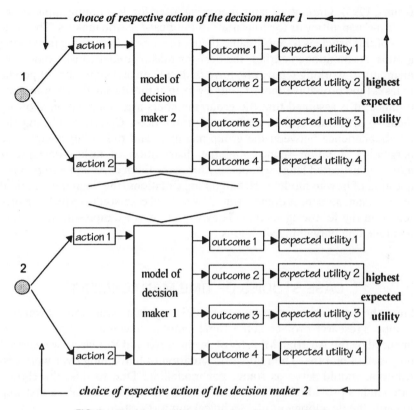

choice of respective action of the decision maker 1

action 1	→	model of decision maker 2	→ outcome 1 → expected utility 1
action 2			→ outcome 2 → expected utility 2 **highest expected utility**
			→ outcome 3 → expected utility 3
			→ outcome 4 → expected utility 4

FIG. 2.   Decision-making process based on game theory.

thinks about goals and possibilities of opponents. As a consequence it must also be made clear what others already have revealed. In other words, a time sequence of who chooses when, who observes whose actions at which point of time must be determined—the rules of the game are essential for any judgement on possible outcomes. This means that the expected behaviour of the opponents is no longer expressed by a probability value but can be described algorithmically (see also Egger & Hanappi, 1995).

Finally, the interdependence of decision makers in game theory formulations enables a more careful treatment of the existing knowledge and memory of the involved parties. Experience and learning now not only consist in the updating of probabilities on the basis of observed data, as is the case in classical decision theory; now knowledge is knowing the models of others and ultimately ascribing probabilities to these models too. Contrary to the classical view, which mainly is preoccupied with one-shot decisions, game theory starts with fully developed entities using their heterogeneous knowledge structures to achieve far-sighted goals (see also

Brams, 1994). Until now, game theory was used for developing applications for firms' consulting or for consulting of political decision makers. The basic idea of this article is to apply game theory to support bargaining in working groups. As mentioned earlier, the decision makers under consideration are members of working teams who have to decide on an assignment of people to tasks (and probably times). Contrary to an authoritarian decision-making instance, it is assumed that the group members are in a position allowing them to articulate and to push their preferences. Clearly modelling the interdependence between the group members and the rather competitive bargaining situation—concerning the distribution of tasks—demands a more sophisticated language, namely for game theory. As a pre-step to the question of how to model such bargaining situations, the "manual" method of time management is demonstrated by several case-studies which are presented in the following section. They will serve as examples in the section on modelling bargaining situations.

CASE-STUDIES OF TIME MANAGEMENT

Since the question emerges how to model bargaining situations of working groups, a research project on the "time-handling of women" (Egger, 1995), financed by the Austrian Ministry of Science, Art and Research, was carried out over 18 months. The real-world situation of bargaining over work distribution should serve as source for modelling. Due to this, the chosen case-studies provide the main features of the model to be built, a first step towards the development of a technical support system.

Method

The project team did an in-depth study of the time-handling practices of four different case-studies. Standard qualitative research methods such as semi-structured interviews and team-meeting observation were used to explore:

- women's time-handling in different organizational settings
- time conflicts emerging from individual preferences and time requirements of the organization
- possible technical support for co-operative time management.

The investigation was done qualitatively by single semi-structured interviews with every group member of the case-studies. During a time period of two hours the group members were asked questions concerning their job as well as their private circumstances. Furthermore, they were asked to draw the "power structure of the group", and a "time-electrocardiogram" of the weekly team day. The time structure of an average day offered insights into events influencing their daily lives. In order to catch an impression of the subjective perception of time, the people were asked to choose one (or more) of the offered "notions" of time (which were selected during pre-tests of the interviews) and to explain their choice: river, swimming pool, key, bag, hammer, corset, and money. Additionally the periodic team meetings were observed. The idea hereby was to get an impression of the bargaining situations in terms of sitting order, the sequence of topics, the number and kinds of verbal interaction, the role of the discussion leader, the "discussion culture", and the extent of participation of the group members.

In order to have an opportunity to compare the specifically-emerging conflicts, the teams were chosen according to their different organizational structures.

- The first group was a feminist consulting office. The political claim of egalitarian decision making and the network structure were the main characteristics.
- A semi-formal hierarchical decision structure with strong informal relations was given in the team of a private research institute (which was of mixed gender).
- The strict hierarchy of a hospital offered two case-studies varying in the applied working time model: one experimenting with a flexible model, the other sticking to the classical shift model.

The Feminist Consulting Group

The consulting office has its seat in Vienna. The feminist group currently consists of eight women (one is on sabbatical leave) where one is some kind of secretary and others are therapists. Three of them founded the investigated consulting office for women in 1979. There is some kind of division into a group of "old members" who joined the consulting office shortly after foundation, and a group of four "young members" who joined during the last four years. All women work for the consulting office for 20–25 hours per week. There exists an internal guideline stating how many clients are to be consulted in a first therapeutic conversation, how many group therapies have to be led, and how many single therapies have to be covered. Due to this guideline each woman has a certain number of female clients, first consulting, etc. Additionally they founded three working groups for internal tasks (public relations, finance, internal organization) and are buying additional external working force (cleaners, computer specialists, doctors, lawyers). They plan their labour for one year. Every woman has the right to formulate working time preferences.

Time-management mainly is done by giving the secretary (who handles all the telephone answering services) reserved time periods, within which

she can make appointments with clients. Extraordinary dates and obligations (invitations to conferences, workshops, etc.) are discussed in the
weekly organizational meeting.

Selected Results of the Empirical Investigation.   The organization does
have some kind of hierarchy (even though some did neglect this in the
interviews), which reflects the duration of the memberships of the women:
The three founding members have most authority. Every woman asked had
the feeling that—except for the secretary—they all have the same rights
concerning time autonomy, self-determination, and decision making.
Nevertheless, a hidden unequal authority distribution seemed to co-exist.
All women are strongly motivated and do experience the group as team
representing common political aims. They attend a monthly supervision
session, in which group-dynamic problems are discussed and reflected.

Each woman assesses time autonomy and time flexibility as very positive.
They can all formulate personal preferences in the planning procedure, the
most severe of which are child care and additional jobs; individual time-
planning mechanisms depend very much on private circumstances: Women
with children structure their days very strongly by time-points, while women
without kids plan with time-intervals. The duration of tasks is estimated
quite accurately if it is routine work; the estimation of new tasks is very
difficult for all women—mostly the duration is underestimated—only one
woman said that she is reserving too much time.

All women say that there is much room for negotiating the distribution
of work. Nevertheless, many find it very tiring to discuss so many things in
principle. They prefer a clear attitude towards the engagement in political
questions. At the moment this kind of discussion only takes place if a certain
event occurs, such as a conference for which it is not clear if somebody of
the consulting office should participate or not. But if additional work has to
be done it could be observed that the women with the "weaker" nerves are
more willing to take it. If nobody has time, this type of labour is not done.

The Private Research Institute

The group of the private research institute consists of 12 persons, where two
are secretaries responsible for all administration jobs. The group of scientific
staff has four men (one is the director) and six women (one is the vice-
director). The underlying decision structure is a semi-formal hierarchy,
where the director and the vice-director are important positions clustering
the scientific staff around them. This is so because most staff members were
recruited by these two persons.

Since the director runs a university institute too (not situated in Vienna),
his presence is limited to two or three days per week. This fact leads to the

phenomenon that the vice-director has much decision competence; only in situations of conflict, is it expected that the director fulfils his role.

The planning group consists of the director, the vice-director, and the secretary, who do not reserve fixed times for planning sessions, but meet "from time to time". The rest of the staff is more involved in carrying out research projects. Since the institute has to finance itself by research projects, quite a high performance pressure exists concerning the necessity of acquiring new projects. Due to this, all (except five persons) are working as freelances for 20–25 hours a week depending on the available research projects. Once every month the group does have a staff meeting for three hours in which all current problems are discussed, and projects are presented.

Selected Results of the Empirical Investigation.   The group members do not experience the team consistently. Some complain about the exclusion of general discussion, such as mid-term planning of projects, and about inappropriate information distribution. One woman did not acknowledge she was part of a team, even though it could be observed that she was co-operating with colleagues in various research projects. There is high pressure to acquire new projects since the economic existence of most staff members cannot be guaranteed. Another difficulty in this group was the fact that different institutions financing projects had different cost guidelines for staff. This means that, for a scientist, payment depended much on the project in which he/she was participating. This lead to a highly conflict-loaded atmosphere, since it was not clear "how much a working hour costs". Nevertheless, all persons liked their jobs, especially because they were offered time autonomy and time flexibility, at least within the time constraints of the granted research projects.

The Nursing Group with the Classical Shift Model

The nursing team of the Viennese hospital consists of 16 persons (13 women and three men). Besides the two head nurses there are seven nurses and seven assistants working on this ward. The investigated group is applying the principle of group nursing, which means (contrary to function nursing) that the staff is split into two working groups each serving half of the patients. Every second day the teams swap patients. By doing so this guarantees that all nurses and assistants know all patients, which is important for night shifts. The working time of the teams is organized in the following shift sequence: two nurses and two assistants work in one shift consisting of two day shifts (12 hours each), followed by one night shift (12 hours), followed by one "sleeping day" and two free days.

Those working outside the shift are working every day from 7AM to 2PM (eventually 3PM). The assignment of the working times to the staff is done by one head nurse; changes between shifts can be made if reported to the head nurse.

There is a daily meeting at 8.45AM in which the doctors are also present to discuss details of the patients' treatment. Additionally the nurses have to attend the doctors' visit. Staff meetings are held once a month or once every two months in which the working hours for the staff are assigned for the next two months.

Selected Results of the Empirical Investigation.   Due to the rather equal distribution of tasks among the nurses and assistants (except if differentiated by law) the team members appreciate the co-operative atmosphere. This induces high motivation for their jobs. It was very interesting that none of the group criticized the shift model. They appreciated very much the mid-term planning perspective which enabled them to plan their private lives, too. Furthermore the long period of rest (one sleeping day and two free days) was experienced as a socially very useful interval of time. The working day is structured by external requirements and often makes an *ad hoc* adjust-ment of the planned sequence of tasks necessary (e.g. the doctors usually don't meet the fixed time-point for the visit, so the nurses have to be quite flexible). While the morning is rather full with various things to do, the afternoon opens up a more flexible and less stressful working atmosphere. The nurses as well as the assistants suffer from the problem that there is little time left over for personal contact with patients or colleagues.

The Nursing Group with the Flexible Time Model

The group consists of 15 persons: two head nurses, nine nurses, and four assistants. The head nurses are working every day from 7AM to 3PM. The four assistants have fixed working times of 43 hours per week (in the form of day shifts); the nurses also have fixed working time of 43 hours, but consisting of day and night shifts.

Work is done by forming two disjunctive staff teams serving half of the patients each. They also apply the model of group nursing, making the whole team responsible for the accomplishment of all necessary tasks.

Every two months there is a planning session of three hours which is used for information distribution and task assignment for the following two months. Additionally, once a month there is a group meeting for group problems and a daily staff meeting including doctors and therapists.

Selected Results from the Empirical Investigations.   Even though the team appreciated the co-operative working atmosphere, it could be observed that the flexible time model induced some conflicting aspects: Almost always the same women (namely the ones avoiding disturbances in the team) took the unwanted working hours. The planning procedure was not experienced as being co-operative, it was mainly a question of speed to get the better dates.

For the women with the worse nerves it happened that there was no continuous shift plan, which made it very difficult for them to make some kind of mid-term planning in their private lives. This led to the strong wish to return to strict shift working times in order to prevent conflicts within the group. The clear shift programme was thought not to disadvantage these women, but would offer clear long-term working plans.

Different labour shifts and packed tasks within working times made it impossible to find time slots for informal meetings or contact.

In summary, it can be stated that the bargaining situations of the presented case-studies were determined very strongly by the underlying organizational structure. The first thing to be mentioned is that each of the studied groups had a different notion of flexibility: The consulting group converted to a strict long-term time plan, which was worked out by every single woman for herself, but within this framework (which offered a long-term planning perspective in the private sphere, too) the women were able to change appointments if necessary. The time-handling of the private research institute was mainly determined by project deadlines and dates of acquisition of projects. Within the project deadlines the staff member could feel free to determine the intensity and speed of work. The nursing group with the shift model seemed not to have any flexibility at all, but the long-term planning enables the nurses and the assistants to change shifts. The nursing group with the flexible time model experienced flexibility in a negative way: The nurses felt they were reserve resources to be used when necessary.

For a more detailed discussion of the case studies see Egger (1995). As far as the topic of the article is concerned, selected citations are used as references when presenting the problems of system designers trying to model bargaining situations.

IMPORTANT ASPECTS OF BARGAINING FOR SYSTEM DESIGN

In order to improve decision-making and bargaining processes, technical systems were and still are developed to support the concerned people. The used approaches base on mainly two views of negotiation: the group-dynamic and the interest-oriented focus. Both are presented briefly in the following.

The basic assumption of theories focusing on group-dynamic negotiation processes is that goodwill, forthright exchanges, and persistence on the part of the negotiators will lead to agreements satisfying all parties; for example, Robey, Farrow, and Franz (1989, p. 1174) focus on managing conflicts and communication in order to achieve "constructive outcomes". The underlying view is that "the preferences of multiple parties can be satisfied with the same solution . . . That is conflict can have constructive outcomes that conflicting parties experience as mutually beneficial". The important aspect of this approach is its emphasis on personal experience which means the individual perception is the key to the agreement on a solution. As a consequence much effort is put on techniques for encompassing the bargaining process (compare e.g. Bertcher, 1994; Forsyth, 1990): The main focus is laid on group-dynamic aspects of individual psychological profiles (such as dominance of single person, outsiders, and the like). It is there where conflicts arise and therefore they have to be solved on this level (Fisher, 1981). It is the respective psychological profile of the group members and not time preferences and qualifications which are responsible for impasses in the negotiation process.

Hiltz, Johnson, and Turoff (1986) try to use information and communication technologies precisely to circumvent the (psychological) dysfunctionality of face-to-face meetings. Kiesler and Sproull (1992) see the same advantages in the depersonalization of computer-mediated bargaining processes, but also point at certain negative effects: group members experience more difficulty in attaining group concensus, and lose feedback regarding the impact of their behaviour on interaction partners, and the like.

Contrary to the first set of bargaining theories, the second set shifts the focus towards time preferences and qualification profiles of group members. Since—in this article—time–tasks–person assignments were considered to be the topic of the bargaining procedure, it is necessary to treat them as the main source of conflict (contrary to the first approach, where psychological profiles are the central source of conflict). Murnighan and Conlon (1991, p. 182) state that "successful groups handled conflict with a variety of strategies that allowed the conflict to continue without being disruptive". Implicitly they assume that there exist conflicts that cannot be solved. This leads to a change in the meaning of negotiation: Bargaining is the struggle of conflicting interests. The solution of this procedure therefore is not any agreement satisfying the group members emotionally, but a compromise acceptable to all group members, knowing that under given circumstances the obtained solution is the best one (compare also e.g. Schelling, 1981). The psychological well-being plays a minor role, especially if—as it often is the case in reality—the bargaining process is constrained in terms of time and outcome by the organizational settings. Another important constraint in the interplay between the negotiating parties is the formal and informal power structure of the organization (Egger & Hanappi, 1994b).

This view of the bargaining process leads us immediately to game theory as the appropriate formal tool: Since a change of assignments for one group member generally induces consequences for other members, too—as long as the group is tightly coupled in the terminology of Perrow (1984)—the utility of a certain assignment of a person depends on the strategic choices of the others. Exactly this interdependence is the characteristic for a successful application of game theory.

Obviously the modelling of a bargaining process needs further specifications. Strauss (1979) offers an inventory of properties according to which a negotiation situation can be characterized. In the following this framework will be applied to bargaining processes over task–time–person assignments. Therefore the next paragraphs are organized along the following lines: The characteristics of a bargaining situation are presented, highlighted by an example of the case-studies, and finally interpreted from a system designer's point of view.

The number of the negotiators, their relative experience in negotiating, and whom they represent.   In our case this is the number of people among whom work is shared; each person represents him/herself. As the case-studies have shown it is quite clear for the concerned people who belongs to the team. Nevertheless there are always people influencing the decision without participating.

> The problem is that we can have a nice working plan, but we cannot be sure when the doctors are making their visit, and, of course, we cannot tell them when to come.
>
> [nursing group with shift model]

Relative experience in bargaining plays a major role, since, e.g. in the case of the nursing group with the flexible model, the more experienced nurses knew ways of getting "good dates". For modelling the bargaining situation in the game theory language, the negotiators are the people making their proposals for task–person assignments. Their experience can be represented explicitly by "strategies" (which can be used for learning, see also Egger, 1996) or are implicitly included in their proposals. In the latter case, experience in negotiating plays a minor role, since a proposal made in a technical system might not necessarily be explained or justified.

The relative balance of power exhibited by the respective parties in the negotiation itself.   Power will be signified by high time autonomy and the possibility to dispose of the time of others. As the case-studies show, even among formally equal group members (e.g. the consulting group) informal power structures emerge.

> Although we are formally equal, the women being the longest time at the consulting office have most power. This can be seen in that they don't need to offer reasons for having no time.
>
> [consulting group]

The influence of power can easiest be modelled by the use of power indices. This means that the proposal of certain group members are weighted. Evidently the modelling of the power structure shows a principal dilemma of system designers: Neglecting formal or informal power distribution leads to unrealistic bargaining tools; considering it could mean fixing the existing power structure.

The clarity of legitimacy boundaries of the issues negotiated.   Besides the group's internal power structure determining the bargaining process, the group usually is embedded in an economic environment which exogenously restricts the scope of negotiable issues; for example the group's tasks, deadlines and times for planning the work distribution and the like are given by an external instance.

> The problem is that I have only a very restricted scope of co-determination, since the general project-schedule is often given by the client and we have to try to realize it. There is not much space anymore.
>
> [research institute]

Modelling those boundaries requires the analysis of the environment determining the bargaining situation. This means that system designers have to put much effort on a thorough analysis of the underlying framework influencing the scope and the kind of bargaining. This would be realized in a technical system by e.g. plausibility checks, which prevent the negotiation of topics which are not under question.

The nature of their respective stakes in the negotiation.   In time–task–person assignments this comes up to a trade-off between time-preferences and preferences for certain types of tasks: When do I prefer to work versus what do I prefer to work at? In the case-studies this was not the main aspect, since it was quite clear what they had to do. A more serious question was the trade-off between participating in the negotiating process and trying to push their own preferences and refusing to articulate their own wishes. This was evident in all case-studies.

> Sometimes I do not have the nerves to fight for a certain shift, even though it would be important for me. I am afraid to get troubles with the others.
>
> [nursing group with flexible model]

These group-dynamic aspects are one of the most serious difficulties for modelling bargaining situations. There are modelling tools (such as e.g. indifference curves) enabling an estimate of the trade-off for the concerned people. Another way to consider this phenomenon would be to allow the negotiators to make "empty entries" in their proposals. Nevertheless, it has to be faced that sometimes the psychological profile of group members plays a crucial role in bargaining situations. From a modelling side it can hardly be expected to be considered, except for simulation games as presented in Egger (1996).

The visibility of transactions to others; that is, their overt or covered character.   The case-studies show very graphically that there is a trade-off between making things visible and hiding them.

> There are many taboos in our group, even though we state to discuss every-thing frankly. I think that we are afraid that too many things start to be questioned. On the other hand I think that clarifying points would decrease stress.
>
> [consulting group]

The essence of the game theory approach is to model exactly this interplay between visible proposals put forward and the hidden strategies in case of conflicts leading to solution proposals. In particular, applied game theory provides a wide spectrum of equilibrium concepts helping to identify con-stellations where negotiations might settle—given strategic competencies and information-processing capacities of the involved persons.

The options of avoiding or discontinuing negotiation; that is, the altern-ative modes of action perceived as available.   In the sense of co-operative decision making it is assumed that there is no alternative to negotiating task–time–person assignments, though there are constraints. Nevertheless, within the group there might well be single group members who are not strongly interested in putting forward their preferences and who therefore are not participating in the bargaining process. In the case-studies all were very interested in attending their planning sessions. Nevertheless, many criticized the psychological effort required to push their own interests. Others questioned the maturity of the group to bargain over task distri-bution.

> I prefer the shift model because the head nurse is doing all the planning decisions. I know that a more flexible model could have advantages, but I doubt that my group is mature enough to be able to negotiate also the con-flicting shifts. I am afraid that this would destroy the cooperative atmosphere.
>
> [nursing group with shift model]

Even though the presented list of Strauss offers an analysing tool for bar-gaining situations, its modelling needs further specification: As one might have observed in the presented checklist a most important point is missing, namely the specification of the rules and mechanisms of the bargaining procedure itself. This is so, because Strauss (1979) rather aimed at the specification of the context than of the core procedure, in order to cover a wide range of different core procedures.

For modelling and supporting a bargaining situation, the rules which should be implemented (such as how many rounds of bargaining, which conflict resolution modes should be offered, how consistent and/or conflicting entries are handled) have to be elaborated by the group. One example of simulating a bargaining situation can be found in Egger (1996). As the examples discussed earlier show, modelling a bargaining situation requires rather deep and detailed studies of the concerned group and its organizational environment. Even though several aspects might be ambiguous (e.g. the power structure), the use of game theory as modelling language offers sophisticated features to support negotiating as well as learning.

CONCLUSION

This article undertook the attempt to present aspects of modelling bargaining situations from a system designer's point of view. Instead of using straightforward optimization theories, a more adequate language, namely the language of game theory, was chosen to describe rather sophisticated phenomena of negotiating processes. This approach allows to consider many interesting group-dynamic aspects emerging in bargaining situations. Strategic behaviour, preferences, power, and interdependencies are only some examples which can be modelled adequately. The empirical cases presented served as examples indicating problems of group members when reflecting their "manual" time management. These studies were necessary to get some insights in planning practices which then can be used as sources for modelling. The technical support of group decision making—such as bargaining over work distribution—seems to become a more and more important question. "Telework", "virtual organization", and "borderless office" are only some examples of future visions which will require adequate models of planning procedures of working groups. From a system designer's point of view bargaining is a multilayered social action. Its modelling asks for a rather intensive investigation of the concerned working group, and furthermore leads to a serious intervention of the system designer. The implementation of certain bargaining rules requires a sequence of organizational decisions the group has to make. Game theory is a language allowing strategic behaviour and group-dynamic aspects to be described. The special point is that it is not used to "objectify" the bargaining situation by modelling an external view. Instead the subjective views and interests are captured. As the selected empirical examples have shown, classical decision theories could not handle the many different aspects of a bargaining situation. Nevertheless, the application of game theory makes the job of a system designer not easier, but it allows the payment of adequate attention to a variety of characteristics of bargaining situations. There remain many open questions, which form important future research questions in the field of computer-supported decision making:

- How are "tasks" and "time-units" identified by group members?
- Which indicators are applied for the division of labour?
- Which parameters determine the sequence of subtasks?
- How is "shared view" of the work to be done developed, and how are conflicts resolved?
- How are individual trade-offs between time-flexibility, income, and task-preferences settled?
- Which mental models of the planning procedure of the working group exist?
- What are the differences in those models, and how can they be used as feedback for improving planning practices?

Recent developments of geographically separated working groups has given rise to many unsolved problems regarding how to support those groups by technical systems:

- How are tasks and time-units identified in a working group which is distributed over several locations with different cultures?
- What conflicts emerge from the geographical separation of the group members?
- How is "team-feeling" developed?
- What impact on the labour process does the asynchronous planning procedure have?
- How do the cultural differences influence co-operation?
- How is a shared language concerning the tasks to be done developed?
- How do individual preferences relate to social/cultural background?
- What consequences can be anticipated for the design of a bargaining tool for distributed working groups?

REFERENCES

Allais, M. (1953). Le comportement de l'homme rationnel devant le risque: critique des postulats et axioms de l'école Americaine. *Econometrica, 21*, 503–546.

Arrow, K.J. (1971). *Essays in the theory of risk-bearing.* Amsterdam, The Netherlands: North-Holland.

Bayes, Th. (1764). Essay towards solving a problem in the doctrine of chances. *Philosophical Transactions of the Royal Society of London*, London.

Bertcher, H. (1994). *Group participation: Techniques for leaders and members.* London: Sage Publications.

Brams, S.J. (1994). *Theory of moves*. Cambridge, UK: Cambridge University Press.

Egger, E. (1995). *Der Umgang von Frauen mit Zeit—Implikationen für die Gestaltung von CSCW-Systemen*. Vienna/Frankfurt/New York: Peter Lang.

Egger, E. (1996). *CSCW: The bargaining aspect*. Vienna/Frankfurt/New York: Peter Lang.

Egger, E., & Hanappi, H. (1994a). *A network talk on CSCW*. Paper presented at the international conference on Operations Research, Berlin.

Egger, E., & Hanappi, H. (1994b). *Multi-criteria decision making in groups: A game-theoretic model*. Paper presented at the international symposium on Human Interaction with Complex Systems, Greensboro.

Egger, E., & Hanappi, H. (1995). *CSCW: Decision theory versus game theory*. Paper presented at the international conference on Industry, Engineering, and Management Systems, Cocoa Beach, Florida.

Fisher, B.A. (1981). *Small group decision making*. Tokyo, Japan: McGraw-Hill.

Forsyth, D. (1990). *Group dynamics* (2nd edn.). Pacific Grove, Calif.: Brooks/Cole.

Gravelle, H., & Rees, R. (1981). *Microeconomics*. London & New York: Longman.

Grundin, J. (1994). Computer-supported cooperative work: History and focus. *Computer, May*, 19–26.

Hiltz, S.R., Johnson, K., & Turoff, M. (1986). Experiments in group decision making. *Human Communication Research, 13*(2), 225–252.

Hirshleifer, J., & Riley, J.G. (1992). *The analytics of uncertainty and information*. Cambridge, UK: Cambridge University Press.

Keynes, J.M. (1921). *A treatise on probability*. London: Macmillan.

Kiesler, S., & Sproull, L.S. (1992). Group decision making and communication technology. *Organizational Behavior and Human Decision Processes, 52*, 96–123.

Kreps, D.M. (1990). *Microeconomic theory*. New York/Toronto/Sydney: Harvester Wheatsheaf.

Murninghan, J.K., & Conlon, D.E. (1991). The dynamics of intense work groups: A study of British string quartets. *Administrative Science Quarterly, 36*, 165–186.

Perrow, C. (1984). *Normal accidents: Living with high-risk technologies*. New York: Basic Books.

Ramsey, F.P. (1931). *The foundations of mathematics and other logical essays*. New York: Harcourt, Brace & Co.

Rapoport, A. (1980). *Mathematische Methoden in den Sozialwissenschaften*. Würzburg/Wien: Physika.

Rhodes, P.C. (1993). *Decision support systems: Theory and practice* (Information system series). Orchards, UK: Alfred Waller.

Robey, D., Farrow, D.L., & Franz, C.R. (1989). Group process and conflict in system development. *Management Science, 35*(10), 1172–1191.

Schelling, T.C. (1981). *The strategy of conflict*. Cambridge, UK: Cambridge University Press.

Shackle, G. (1949). *Expectation in economics*. Cambridge, UK: Cambridge University Press.

Strauss, A. (1979). *Negotiations*. San Francisco, Calif.: Jossey-Bass.

EUROPEAN JOURNAL OF WORK AND ORGANIZATIONAL PSYCHOLOGY, 1996, 5 (3), 457–464

Book Reviews

West, M.A., & Farr, J.L. (Eds.). (1991). *Innovation and creativity at work*. Chichester, UK: John Wiley. Pp. 364. ISBN 0-471-93187-X. £22.50.

The book deals with various topics that are interesting to work and organization psychologists, especially to those engaged in organizational development projects.

It is a monograph that consists of five parts. Part One is concerned with problems of definitions, and the general background to research on innovation at work (definitional issues as well as a review of the literature). The importance of the difference between innovation at various levels of organization is stressed: at the individual, the group, and at the level of the whole organization. Each level needs different approaches and research tools for analysis.

Part Two offers a new model for understanding innovation on an individual level. We have here the depiction of the studies of group innovation in established/mature institutions. Also, another important study is presented in this part, namely innovation and creativity among research and development teams.

Part Three is mainly devoted to the analysis of organizational-level innovation. This area of investigation needs a broad scope, both because of the different types of innovation as well as the importance of the integration of the structure, strategy, and environment into the complex innovation model. We receive deep insights into the hidden assumptions and how they act in determining the directions and outcomes at work.

Part Four focuses on interventions directly in work settings, examining the question of how to utilize psychological knowledge to change attitudes as well as to improve communication.

It is intriguing that ideas from developmental psychology are applied to promote innovation in work settings. The interesting proposal is the management method for answering important questions regarding innovation and creativity at work.

Part Five of the book presents a model of individual creativity and organizational innovation, combining psychological and organizational approaches.

The general aims of this book are:

- to define what is meant by innovation and creativity at work
- to illustrate interventions to facilitate innovation at the work site
- to present an accessible overview of existing research in the area
- to present models of innovation and creativity at work
- to integrate the ideas and experiences of researchers and practitioners
- to combine the ideas of researchers from America and Europe.

The most interesting chapter, at least for me, as a work and organizational psychologist, is that presented by J.L. Farr and C.M. Ford (Chapter 10). It concerns the model of individual innovation, including perceptions of the need for change, perceived payoff from change, self-efficacy, and technical knowledge. All four influenced the role of innovation. Many of the ideas presented are consistent with expectancy theory. The authors think that emphasizing the motivational and skill-related aspects of individual innovation may provide an impetus for developing more prescriptive statements regarding this process.

   The book would be of assistance to psychologists, researchers, and practitioners.

ZOFIA RATAJCZAK
Universytet Slaski
Katowice, Poland

Howard, A. (Ed.). (1995). *The changing nature of work*. San Francisco: Jossey-Bass. Pp. 590. ISBN 0-7879-0102-4.

This book is published as part of the "Frontiers of Industrial and Organizational Psychology" series, sponsored by the American Psychological Association. Its objective is to rethink the psychology of work. It analyses the future of working, as information technology, global competition, and the quest for efficiency and flexibility rapidly displace jobs and workers. Ann Howard has brought together a fine group of authors, not only from the field of work and organizational psychology, but also from related areas such as sociology, technology, economics, and industrial relations. As the Preface puts it, it is not a handbook, but still necessarily broad. The book and the writers focus particularly on change, "less on what we know, than what we need to know" (p. xv).

   Howard has managed to integrate the very diverse contributions into a framework that is clarifying without being too restrictive or normative. This framework perceives "work", "workers", and "working" as the core elements of the world of work. These core elements are radically changed by two primary drivers, on the one hand technological and market changes and on the other demographic/social changes. Technological changes stimulate the demand side, i.e. what needs to be done and how. Demographic and social changes influence the supply side, i.e. the kind of workers available. Since the book is aimed at the implications for work and organizational psychology, major issues discussed are issues of selection, training, motivation, job design, teamwork, and other aspects of the human resources area.

The impacts of both of these two major change forces are mediated by governmental policy and (inter)organizational structures and strategies. Finally the interaction between all these forces takes place in a larger political, economic, and societal context.

In Chapter 1, Howard shows the usability of this general framework by describing, in terms of its central concepts, three key periods in American history: industrialization around the turn of the century, the flowering of bureaucracy following World War II, and (the beginnings of) the post-industrial information age since the last decade.

The book is built up around the core issues. The first part explores the framework and the wider political, economic, and societal context. The next three parts are devoted to: (1) work—changes in work and tasks through new technologies, both in manufacturing and in the office; (2) workers—the (mis)match between existing and required education and skills, new selection and placement methods, changing individual–organization attachments, and careers as lifelong learning; and (3) working—teamwork crossing organizational boundaries, leadership, and performance appraisal.

In the final part, the major ideas and conclusions of the previous chapters are brought together and interpreted in a framework derived from complexity theory.

The sections of the book are now discussed in detail.

Part One: The Political Context

In the first part, Howard characterizes the changes in industrial relations in the USA. Wever analyses the large differences between labour relations in the US (low labour-cost oriented) vs Germany (high-skill, high-wage oriented) and Poland (rapidly changing from centralized to Western). He concludes that in all three countries, as in many other industrialized countries, government, business, and organized labour are challenged to restructure the institutions of employment relations towards more flexibility, and towards decentralizing the role of negotiations. Finally, Ledvinka discusses three recent legal developments in the US—the 1991 Civil Rights Act, the Americans with Disabilities Act, and the anti-testing initiatives—and their implications for work psychologists.

Part Two: Work

Van der Spiegel illustrates how computing is now entering a second era, evolving from a tool of computation to a tool of communication. Coovert describes innovations in the area of office technologies. He argues that office tasks will change considerably through the introduction of technologies for "computer supported co-operative work" (groupware), "augmented reality", and "ubiquitous computing" methods. The introduction of these technologies will also require new methods for, among others, training, which in its turn can greatly be supported by the new technologies.

Davis shows that the growth in information and communication technologies, together with two other major trends—growth in knowledge and globalization—results in "boundaryless organizations", i.e. the breakdown of traditional barriers within and between organizations: between groups/ departments, levels of authority, the organization and its suppliers, customers and competitors, work and home, permanent and temporary employees, time periods, etc.

Wall and Jackson critically analyse the traditional psychological approaches to job design, particularly in the context of three new manufacturing technologies and methods: just-in-time logistics, total quality management, and advanced manufacturing technology (e.g. robotics and numerically controlled machines). The Job Characteristics Model of Hackman and Oldham, and the Sociotechnical Systems Perspectives, have provided major theories and concepts underlying modern job design. Autonomy (autonomous work groups), skill variety, and task significance have been considered major determinants of motivation as the prime dependent variable. Wall and Jackson argue that, in the future, organization and job, cognitive demand, production responsibility, and work-interdependence will become at least as important as design parameters. These factors not only determine motivation, but are particularly relevant for knowledge-based mechanisms such as learning, action planning, and error anticipation. These mechanisms thereby increase the feeling of mastery, which makes the individual more resistant to the stressful demands of many modern jobs.

Part Three: Workers

Howard presents an overview of the major demographic changes: increasing age, immigration, changes in the proportions of ethnic grouping, increasing female participation, pressure for participation of disabled people, and the increasing gap between highly skilled and lower skilled people (in the USA, more than in other countries) coupled with a lack of training for the low skilled; this last trend threatens to result in society becoming two-tiered.

The youth labour market is surveyed in more depth by Osterman. He concludes that in all countries youth are first marginalized and later integrated. However, this process is becoming more difficult to manage. He advises therefore: keep youth in school longer and at the same time connect them to the labour market earlier. Carnevale observes that in Europe and Asia non-college youth get better schooling than in the US. However, in all countries the new type of work requires different forms of training, i.e. learning to learn instead of learning a job. In-company training has to change in accordance with this principle. Employees need to be trained in handling responsibilities, interacting with customers, setting and achieving goals, etc.

Landy and associates discuss modern developments in selection and placement methods and compare them to what is required in the future. They point to the following needs:

- Job analysis should concentrate more on attributes than on tasks.
- Special attention should be given to the analysis of team functioning, i.e. group composition, group processes and performance, and on team skills as selection criteria.
- More predictors should be found in information-processing abilities.

Rousseau and Wade-Benzoni analyse the changing individual–organization attachments in modern loosely coupled, flexible and adhocratic organizations. They distinguish between two basic dimensions, resulting in four types of employment relations: short- or long-term connections and outsider–insider connections. Within each of these four categories, both fulltimers and part-timers can be found. Each of these types of employee has different involvement in and commitment to the organization. How to manage these attachments and motivate people is a major challenge for organizational psychologists.

Hall and Mirvis focus on careers. They start from the observation that the time when careers consisted of upward moves within a framework of long-term employment relations has passed. A new strategy of career development should be envisaged, which they call the "protean career" (from the Greek god Proteus, who could change shape at will)—a process that the person, not the organization, is managing. It consists of all the person's varied experiences in education, training, work in several organizations, changes in occupational field, and so forth. This type of career has, among others, the following characteristics:

- permanently learning new skills
- adaptability and change of fields

- lateral rather than upward movement
- continual networking
- personal control.

Organizations should also change their practices and provide information, learning opportunities, and experiences to support these careers.

Part Four: Working

"When People Get Out of the Box" is a chapter by Mohrman and Cohen on work situations that are truly non-bureaucratic and fluid. These organizations appear to be largely team based and place heavy emphasis on lateral interaction and collaboration. Three types of ability are required: (balanced) task and team abilities (e.g. co-operative planning and decision making); cognitive abilities such as the ability to learn and understand different ideas; and commitment. The principle of teamwork does not imply that people are locked permanently in the same group. Employees are members of different teams, experience multiple reporting relationships, and at times take on (quasi)managerial roles. A major challenge for psychologists is to develop insight into the functioning of these fluid peer and managerial relationships, to develop new performance management systems (see also Hedge and Borman), and to design information systems facilitating collaborative work.

The issue of performance appraisal is discussed in detail by Hedge and Borman. They present a general overview of developments in this area. More specifically they discuss the possibilities and merits of electronic performance monitoring and of team appraisal. The characteristics required for leaders in modern organizations are identified by House. These include vision, self-sacrifice, risk taking, development orientation, and role modelling. Apart from these leader behaviours, a number of managerial behaviours are required, such as environmental monitoring, shared strategy formulation, and management of infrastructure.

Finally, Hage discusses the characteristics of post-industrial society in general and the signs of "role failures" (crimes, broken marriages, single-parent raised children, poverty) in the community and family in particular. he argues that we must understand the new demands of post-industrial society, such as: the change towards mental rather than physical activities; the intensity of interactions in all spheres of life; and the changes and inter-penetration of work, family, and leisure roles, which imply that people must learn to live in complex role sets, and in which negotiations about role expectations or behaviour are very crucial. Furthermore, one has to adjust to constant changes in society. People therefore need to have complex and creative (more than intelligent) minds, be adaptive and flexible and know how to understand symbolic (i.e. non-verbal) communications.

Epilogue

In the final chapter, Howard brings all the strands of thought together. She succeeds not only in summarizing the common threads and major lines of argument, but even in integrating these in a theoretical framework derived from "complexity theory". This theory, related to chaos theory, maintains:

> that individual components interact according to a few simple rules. The system operates from the bottom up without a central controller, but a global property emerges and feeds back to influence the behaviour of the individual components. . . . Complex systems evolve through self-organization and selection to what is called the edge of chaos . . . a point of maximal differentiation and integration. (p. 516)

Work organizations in the future will be like complex systems in this sense: complex, fluid, information processing, uncertain, interconnected, invisible. The central question is: how can an equilibrium be maintained at the edge of chaos? The answer is: only if workers are differentiated, creative, adaptable, responsible, and growing; and if working is characterized by empowerment, learning, and interdependence.

Many problems could surface: feelings of insecurity, stress, social friction. But work could also provide compensations: challenge, creativity, flexibility, control, and inter-relatedness. There is a big challenge for organizational psychologists to maximize these potential benefits and prevent the above-mentioned problems from becoming destructive.

The above-presented short description of the various contributions and messages in this book may sometimes give the impression of big words without much substance. Indeed, in some chapters sweeping generalizations abound and concrete illustrations are scarce. The failures of the present-day economic system and of traditional organizational forms and functioning are substantiated with many facts: growing unemployment and too much work for the employed; feelings of uncertainty; trends towards the two-tiered society, etc. But empirical evidence of the success, both for organizations and for workers, of the approaches advocated in this volume is indeed limited. Another point of criticism could be the rather strong USA-orientation. Only one chapter is written by non-Americans (Wall and Jackson). Some other chapters refer to industrial relations in non-American countries but, generally speaking, non-USA phenomena (e.g. concerning institutionalized consultation) and theories which receive much attention in Europe (e.g. socio-technics or decision-making theories) are very difficult to find.

Finally, the projections of future technological systems (e.g. augmented reality or ubiquitous computing in the office), of organizational developments (e.g. the virtual organization), or the role of the individual (e.g. the "protean career") are sometimes rather speculative. However, this is inevitable in a time of turbulent change, in which new forms and instruments are only slowly emerging and hardly yet reported on. Nevertheless, the book presents an impressive overview of the major future issues in the field of organizational psychology, showing the phenomena that have to be dealt with, the research questions that have to be answered, the weaknesses of present models and instruments, and the need for—and sometimes building blocks of—new models and instruments.

Howard and the other contributors have done what they promised: focusing "less on what we know than what we need to know" (p. xv). Of course, many data and conclusions are well known. But the book presents additional information, models to integrate the widely divergent phenomena, and ideas about how to approach these phenomena. It does not minimize the many problems that society will face, or the insecurity that many will encounter, both unemployed and employed. It argues convincingly, however, that solutions can only be found through a radical new approach to working.

J.H. ERIK ANDRIESSEN
Delft University of Technology
The Netherlands